True Riders on the Roads of China

Kirill Luchkin

Published by Kirill Luchkin, 2024.

While every precaution has been taken in the preparation of this book, the publisher assumes no responsibility for errors or omissions, or for damages resulting from the use of the information contained herein.

TRUE RIDERS ON THE ROADS OF CHINA

First edition. April 18, 2024.

Copyright © 2024 Kirill Luchkin.

ISBN: 979-8224210237

Written by Kirill Luchkin.

A FEW WORDS TO START WITH

On a cold winter day in Beijing, after having lived in China for three years, I was struck by the idea of bicycling to the famous Buddhist Yungang Grottoes. It was to be a sort of pilgrimage, where the challenging journey itself was a trial. The round trip from Beijing to those Grottoes and back is no less than 700 miles.

Of course, for such an endeavor, you need a reliable friend, and I have one. As a Chinese song goes, "If we go, we go; there's you and there's me—what more do we need?" This marked the beginning of our bicycle tours across Northern China, where over the years we covered thousands of miles on the roads and mountains of the country.

Back then, there were neither GPS navigators, mobile phones, nor the internet; all over China, only the beep of pagers could be heard. We had only a poor-quality map in our hands and unstoppable adventurous spirits in our heads. Throughout our travels, we didn't encounter a single comrade-in-arms on the roads and realized that we were actually pioneers of bicycle touring in China.

Mountain bicycles were just becoming popular and were considered a luxury item in China. The fortunate few who owned them proudly rode around Beijing, catching envious glances, never even considering heading into the mountains that surround the capital on three sides. We, then students, had to assemble our bicycles ourselves, scavenging for parts from who knows where.

On the roads and in the mountains, we faced grueling ascents and snow-blocked passes, black dust from coal routes, and rocky gorges where we had to carry our faithful steel steeds on our backs. But we were happy on these roads and in these mountains. The crazy descents, where only the wind whistled in our ears, turned into a kind of meditation, healing our souls and making up for hours of difficult climbing. After all, two-thirds of China's territory is mountainous. The goal of all our trips was one sacred mountain or another Buddhist monastery.

This book is a truthful account of our hikes, describing the nuances, experiences with local populations in rural China where our routes took us, dangers, and mysterious incidents we encountered along the way. At the same time, it is a practical guide to bicycle touring and extreme biking in China for anyone who wishes to follow our example and test themselves. Despite the passing years, the basic things described here remain relevant.

Be patient while reading about some technical details on the first pages. I simply cannot omit them. From them, you will be able to feel how we learned firsthand what mountain bike was like. Further on, you will be able to experience what we went through on our hikes, learn about our mistakes, and avoid them if you dare to set out on your steel steed to Northern China. Good luck on the roads and in the mountains.

MOUNTAIN BIKING GEAR
FOR THE TRUE RIDER

Paramount, of course, is the steel steed itself. For a serious journey in China, a bicycle must undoubtedly be of the mountain variety. Contrary to popular saying, this set of two wheels was a relatively recent reinvention - in the 1970s in the US. It differs from the standard bicycle in the following key features:

1/ The presence of multiple drive and driven sprockets, allowing for various torque outputs, and a gear shifting system - moving the chain from one sprocket to another (sport bikes also have multiple sprockets - but usually only driven ones, and fewer than on a mountain bike). A standard mountain bike usually has three drive sprockets and seven driven ones, yielding twenty-one speeds. For descents and climbs, smooth roads and off-road - there are specific speeds. This enables climbing a 30-degree slope on a mountain bike with moderate effort, and with some force - even steeper, crossing over large boulders.

2/ Mountain bike wheels are somewhat smaller in diameter than standard ones - this facilitates overcoming surface irregularities. Tires are 1.5 times wider than standard and thicker, with prominently protruding treads - a true rider travels on various surfaces: soil, rocks, frozen mountain riverbeds, etc. Often, to reduce weight, fenders are absent - fitting the dry, sparse rainfall climate of Northern China - or light plastic mudguards are installed.

3/ A special frame design, considering the frequent inclined position of the athlete's body when moving on sloped terrain, and allowing to avoid an unpleasant impact on the frame, if the athlete slides forward off the saddle during sudden braking, especially when descending a slope.

A mountain bike should be as light as possible, since there may be sections in the mountains where the athlete will have to carry the

"

bike, and not on a flat surface, but while scrambling uphill (sometimes such sections can be quite long). A good mountain bike can easily be lifted onto the shoulder with one hand. In 1994, at the "Arms and Conversion" exhibition in Russia, an American company showcased their mountain bikes (whose manufacturing complexity may be comparable to some types of weapons production). As an advertisement, the Americans suspended a bike frame on a scale - it weighed only a few hundred grams - because it was made of titanium alloy.

In regular production mountain bikes, the frame is of course not made of titanium, but of steel or, on good bikes, of strong aluminum alloy. In any case, it's lighter than that of a standard bike (with the exception, and not an isolated one, of poor-quality mountain bikes - see below). Other parts are made of various aluminum alloys and plastics, except for the most critical ones - axles, pedal cores - those are steel.

4/ At the same time, a mountain bike must be very sturdy, as it endures far more significant stresses than a standard one. Frequent transfer of the entire body weight onto one pedal, constant sharp braking, impacts against stones, blows from flying stones, intense vibration during fast descent on a rocky slope - all this a mountain bike must withstand. Hydraulic shock absorbers on the front fork are extremely desirable - it is the front that takes on the main stress during sharp braking or when the front wheel hits a stone (some bikes are equipped with both front and rear shock absorbers).

5/ A mountain bike is also sometimes equipped with special accessories, among which are the so-called "horns". These are two curved forward and upward aluminum tubes, protruding at the ends of the handlebar, which indeed resemble bull horns. What are they for? Firstly, "horns" prevent the athlete's hands from slipping off or being thrown from the handlebar due to strong shaking, impact, which are constant when moving in the mountains. Secondly, they protect the hands when the athlete brushes the handlebar against an obstacle (for example, a rock). Additionally, during long ascents, when you often have to push the bike uphill for hours, it's convenient to hold it by the "horns" - it changes the body angle and the back experiences less fatigue.

It's very important to adjust the angle of the "horns" correctly, otherwise, they can do more harm than good. If the "horns" are bent too much upwards, instead of sliding off when hitting an obstacle, they will catch on it. This is relevant even in urban conditions. When moving at high speed (as a true rider, who believes that brakes were invented by cowards, does) through a street in Beijing, weaving through the chaos of cars, motorcycles, bicycles, rickshaws, pedestrians, you often need to squeeze, say, between a "box"[1] and a daydreaming pedestrian on the road. In such a case, you might slightly brush the "horn" against the daydreamer. And here, if your "horn" is improperly set, it will definitely catch on the clothing or, say, the strap of the shoulder bag of the daydreamer, resulting in an accident.

In general, for overcoming mountains and traveling hundreds of miles, the bike must be meticulously adjusted. To avoid muscle pain from an unfortunate body position, it's essential to precisely position, adjusted to one's height, the handlebar and saddle - this is the ABC of cycling. All rotating parts must rotate freely, providing the minimum force re- quired, but without play. It's also very important to thoroughly clean the chain with alcohol (or WD-40) and lubricate it. But the main thing - impeccably adjusted brakes (as one's life often depends on them).

One should not forget about such a seemingly unnecessary thing in the mountains as a horn (in recent years, air horns have replaced bicycle bells). In the mountains, there are villages. I remember, trying to reach Sheng Tang Bao, Shanxi province, by midnight, we were rapidly descending in the darkness down a road somewhere between villages of Quhuisi and Sanlou. The flashlight batteries were dead, it was a moonless night, and we navigated only by the vague outlines of the poplars growing along the roadside. Suddenly, right in front of me, something black swiftly appeared. I managed to brake sharply, simultaneously veering to the left. It was apparently a local peasant. What devil drove him to travel at such a late hour, when all decent people are at home, along this road without a flashlight?! A similar question arose, apparently, for the peasant, as he shouted something after us in an incomprehensible local dialect and even tried to catch up. We had no time to waste explaining things to him and were soon far away. However, we continued the descent, constantly sounding the horn (for some reason, I was reminded of the "Titanic").

Now, about choosing a bicycle. It must be a reliable steel steed, not just any tub. Therefore, it is not recommended to go to the mountains on a Chinese bicycle (i.e., one where all or most, or some, but crucial parts are made in the PRC). Although in Beijing, where shifu[2] sit on every corner, it's quite possible to ride one. The main flaw of Chinese bicycles is the extremely low quality of steel used for manufacturing key parts: under any serious load, pedals break off, frames bend, threads strip.

The best mountain bikes in Asia and their parts are made in Japan. Perhaps the best that can be bought in Beijing are Taiwanese models, but such a purchase is not cheap - up to 4,000 USD (for this money, you can buy several cheap motorcycles or a used car here). Therefore, the best practical choice is a bike assembled from parts of various origins: a Chinese frame, made under the CATIC firm's license, Taiwanese handlebar and saddle KALIN, the most responsible parts are Japanese: bottom bracket SAKAE, gear shifters, chain, hubs SUNTOUR or SHIMANO, wheels ARAYA, pedals MKS, WELLGO, brakes DIA-COMPE, shock absorbers TOSHI.

This way you can embark on a hundred miles, to the mountains, taking with you just a couple of necessary wrenches, glue, and patches in case of a tire puncture.

On my first trip, not having any experience yet, I went on the bike that I had. It was a sports road model produced at the Kharkiv Bicycle Factory in Ukraine, to which I gave the name Arctic Fox (every true rider, loving and caring his steel steed, gives it a name). I rode the Arctic Fox 700 miles without a single breakdown (except for a stone knocked out spoke that wrapped around the rear hub). But the gear lever was positioned on it so that you had to take your right hand off the handlebars to reach it - unless you hit a pothole or a rock - and if you managed to hold the bike with one hand, you were just lucky. The Arctic Fox has still managed to cope with the descent of Kongjian, but, say, in the Long Men gorge, it is useless. So, I soon replaced Arctic Fox with a mountain Wildcat, and Victor initially had a mountain Ji Kong, which he then changed to Diamond Ass.

A mountain biker packs his gear in a small backpack, which must be securely tied to the luggage rack. By the way, riding a bicycle over more or less long distances with a back- pack on your shoulders is absolutely unprofessional. We won't go into detail about the backpack's contents, only noting that it's small, as we never took a food supply with us on the bike tour (why - see below). It's also worth mentioning that there's no point in going on a bike tour without a map, a knife, and a flashlight (it's good if the latter combines with a taser). The knife will be needed for opening and eating canned peaches, as well as in case of a leopard attack. The flashlight is needed to illuminate the map at night.

A bit more about Chinese maps. Satellites have been flying in the sky for many years, photographing even Mars and Venus, but in China, you won't find sufficiently large-scale and detailed maps for sale. The most detailed maps available for sale are designed for motorists, so only roads suitable for cars are marked on them. But don't think that all car roads are marked, or that they are marked accurately. The main principle when dealing with a Chinese map (as well as with tourist guides, atlases, etc.) is don't believe your eyes. Where the map shows a straight stretch of road, you will find a winding serpent or several intersections. To this, add that there is a complete lack of a sign system on the roads of the Celestial Empire. The existing signs are random, moreover, locals somehow like to turn them around or move them, disorienting travelers. Therefore, navigation in the field during a trek can be greatly complicated - and what consequences this can lead to!

If you've heard of the most famous travel guides for countries and cities of the world by the Australian publishing house "Lonely Planet" and think that a guide from this respectable publisher will definitely help you on a trek, you are sorely mistaken. Firstly, there are no sufficiently detailed maps in "Lonely Planet" books. Secondly, they are designed for "moral freaks" (tourists)[3], moreover, pampered by civilization, for whom an adventure is already simply to ride a minibus next to a mountain (as we learned from the "Lonely Planet" guide to China). In general, it should be noted that mountain biking is a very special activity, the adherents of which are apparently few (at least, in China, over the years and thousands of miles, we have never met a single brother-in-arms), and therefore don't hope to find suitable guides or tourist handbooks for it.

In conclusion, a few words about the attire of a true rider. Practice teaches to wear several layers of clothing (from 2-3 in summer to 5-6 in winter) so that by taking off and put- ting it on in due time, you can regulate the temperature. This is related to frequent and sharp temperature fluctuations during the tour: during the day in the mountains under the sun, it is hot even in winter, at night it is cold even in summer; while moving, especially uphill, the body heats up greatly, but once you stop and if it's cold, you immediately start freezing. As for footwear, it must be suitable for climbing exercises - i.e., the soles should not slip when you are scrambling up a rock or, say, moving on an icy-snowy slope.

The tactics of our journey are dictated by the Chinese specifics. You've probably heard that China is densely populated, and indeed, the land here is almost entirely developed and inhabited. However, it's worth clarifying: by whom and how.

It is known that majority of China's population are peas- ants. And it is they who, over 3,000 years, have cultivated and populated the area through which our journey passes. This is evident in the presence of fields, garden plots, terraces, sheep and villages along the entire route, stretching for hundreds of miles (except for mountain passes, where it is impossible to live or grow anything). The rural area starts immediately at the outskirts of the city, soon becoming denser, the villages smaller and the distances between them greater, up to places where electricity has not yet been installed and where it is impossible to travel even by bicycle.

Yet, even a glance at a Chinese map will convince you that wherever you go, you are always within a few dozen miles of some village. Add to this that in any of these villages (with rare exceptions), a late traveler can find food and lodging (we will talk more about the Chinese village below). For a true rider, even at night or in the mountains, covering a few dozen miles on a steel steed, especially when hungry, is no trouble at all. This is why, when setting out, we never took with us either a supply of food or, moreover, a tent. This allowed us to lighten our equipment as much as possible, which is very important for runs of hundreds of miles, and especially for crossing various passes and ravines.

Hence, the tactics of our journeys are as follows: move the maximum possible distance during the day, and with the onset of night, look for lodging at one of the nearest points. The most important thing in such tactics is to know when to stop. We learned this lesson during our very first harsh Datong trek. We set out for Datong city, to the famous Yungang Grottoes, in cold December. After about 30 miles, we decided to rest and snack in the village of Qingbaikou, where we were brazenly tried to be overcharged at a roadside tavern. Needless to say, the swindlers didn't get a single extra mao[4] from us, but a very unpleasant impression remained, and who knew then what consequences it could lead to!

It was already dark when the road began to rise slightly but steadily upwards. A bit tired after 75 miles traveled in a day, we hurried on. Soon in the darkness on the left, the out- lines and rare lights of some village appeared. According to the map, this should have been a village of Little Dragon's Gate, immediately after it was Linchang, or Forest Place, and a few miles further – Kongjian village. It wasn't even 11 o'clock in the evening, and calculating the distance, we decided to go to Kongjian to spend the night there. And so, when we had almost passed the dark Little Dragon's Gate, in the penultimate house facing the road, we saw a light. It was nothing other than the only roadside inn here. The curtained windows indicated that the establishment was closed, but the owners were still awake.

At first, we didn't even stop at the inn, but after walking another 50 steps, we suddenly felt thirsty and decided to stop by this light in the hope of at least drinking a cup of green tea.

Upon knocking, the door immediately opened, and the owner appeared at the threshold, warmly inviting us inside. When we sat down at the table, we suddenly felt a bit hungry and, looking at the blackboard on the wall with chalk-written names of simple dishes with very modest prices, unheard of by Beijing standards, we decided not to refuse the offered dinner. A couple of minutes later, eating huge bowls of noodles with meat and a dish of tofu, we talked with the friendly owner and his respectable wife, trying to find out as much as possible from them about the road ahead.

According to the owner, "foreign devils" had appeared in these parts only once before - it was a certain lost German guy driving a jeep, who turned back from Little Dragon's Gate to Beijing. Learning about our destination - the distant Yungang Grottoes - the owner was quite surprised, and immediately told us that right after their village begins a large mountain, where, moreover, leopards live (these, as is known, are most active at the onset of darkness). We remembered that shortly before it got dark, we met a lone peasant walking with a long, two-meter, air gun on his shoulder. "Just a couple of months ago, two of our guys went with guns to hunt a leopard, but they were unlucky. The leopard ate them. And they were both not even 40 years old yet!" - the owner sighed.

If you think that all this caused us some concern, then you don't yet know about the power of the thrill of moving forward. The desire to continue the journey strengthened even more when the owner passionately tried to persuade us to spend the night with him - here we involuntarily remembered Qingbaikou, where they tried to cheat us, and a suspicion crept into our hearts that the cunning owner was trying to earn more from us. While he was quite plausibly describing the height of the mountain ahead, it seemed to us that he was deliberately exaggerating to make us stay and take money from us not only for dinner but also for lodging and breakfast. Little did we know then that Deng Xuchen, who would later become simply Dage (Elder Brother) to us, with whom we can now find shelter at any hour of the day or night, even without a single penny in our pocket, had been a fair and honest man since his youth. And yet, at the last moment, when we were already about to get up from the table, *something* made us change our minds and agree to stay in Small Dragon's Gate for the night.

Dage's father, the old man, appeared. There was some- thing in his face that was not peasant-like. Later, we saw in the fanza[5] a large frame on the wall with family photographs, where in one of them the old man in his youth was captured in the uniform of a Kuomintang army officer, and everything became clear. Along the narrow, stone streets of the village, no more than a meter wide, which went slightly uphill, the old man led us in complete darkness to the fanza. Then he personally lit the kang[6] in the vacant room for us. Dage and his wife used to live here before they moved to the inn they had opened. While the room was airing out from the smoke, the old man invited us to sit in the next room, where on another huge kang, Dage's old mother and daughter, a visiting nephew, and a cat were already lying in clothes under thick cotton blankets.

Soon after our bodies touched the kang, we fell asleep. The truth began to dawn on us in the morning when the wind woke us up, having flung open the door shutters and burst into the room. Going out into the yard, and visiting its corner, where next to the pen with a huge pig sitting in it, there was a pit that we had already visited the evening before, we discovered that the air was somehow too clean and fresh, and in the west the village was surrounded on all sides by mountains rising up.

After feeding us breakfast, Dage asked us for only a symbolic sum, and we realized that we had been wrong in our suspicions the night before. Here we developed the deepest respect for him, just as he was amazed by our intention to reach the Yungang Caves on steel steeds, and at Dage's suggestion, we became sworn brothers. Then we took a photo with Dage and his family: grandfather, wife, and five-year-old daughter, using a Ricoh camera. This shot, like another one taken by us later, was subsequently placed by Dage in the family frame. Thanking Dage wholeheartedly and saying our warm goodbyes, we set off.

We didn't get on our steel steeds until almost noon - the road went so steeply uphill that we could only move on foot. Now we know that it was the Kongjian Pass. Only there did we fully understand what we had avoided the night before by staying with Dage. We spent half a day on an exhausting climb. Many places looked like a leopard could jump on us from above right now, in daylight. Linchang, Forest Place, turned out not to be a village, but a deserted forest station where we definitely could not have expected to find shelter. At the highest point of the pass, which is the border between the Beijing municipality[7] and Hebei province, the wind whistled and our hands froze from the cold, from the same place the paved road ended and we long descended down a steep, stony serpentine road, bordered on one side by cliffs and on the other by precipices hundreds of feet high. Only around two in the afternoon did we descend into Kongjian village. What would have happened to us if we had continued our journey the night before, one can only guess, but certainly nothing good. The lesson was learned, but still, a few years later, succumbing to an inexplicable thrill, we broke the golden rule - to stop in time - and the consequences were much more serious this time. But we won't talk about that yet.

One might wonder: wouldn't it be better to mark a destination on the map in advance, say, a certain village, reach it and stop there? Perhaps it would be, but the trouble is, it's impossible. Let's explain why.

Some 70% of China's territory is mountainous. Therefore, even a trek whose ultimate goal is not a mountain will still pass through mountains. Even when moving through a mountain valley on what seems to be a flat road, over time you notice that the road is actually inclined in one direction or another.

Movement in the mountains has its own rules. Information that it's, say, five miles from one point to another carries no specific meaning here - because five miles can sometimes be covered in 15 minutes, and sometimes in two hours. In mountaineering, for example, distance is always measured in hours. They say: it's five hours from here to such-and-such a pass, not ten miles (only when a mountaineer is climbing a sheer cliff do they say, for example, that this rock wall is 100 feet high).

For this reason, knowing, for example, that we've traveled from Beijing to Wutai Mount about 250 miles, it's futile to compare this with the distance from, say, Miami to St. Petersburg, because 250 miles through the flat as a table Florida and through Chinese mountains and passes are entirely different things.

Setting out on a journey, a true rider always moves along a new, unknown route. He relies only on the Chinese map, which contains no information about altitude differences, showing only the highest peaks starting from 1,000 feet. Therefore, he always faces the unknown - how much time will be needed to cover the intended distance and where he will find himself at a certain hour (it is for this reason that one often has to move at night).

Some experience with Chinese maps allows predicting the presence of mountains and passes ahead. Suppose you see on the map a point named Lower Stone Fortress, and ahead - another point named Upper Stone Fortress, then undoubtedly, an ascent lies before you. Names like Cloudy Ridge, High Gates etc., are ominous. Moreover, if you notice that the road on the map begins to twist like a snake, you can be sure that soon you will have to climb a steep mountain via a serpentine road.

Yet, often a mountain appears before you without any signs of its presence on the map. And even if you suspect its appearance, you still don't know how steep and long the as- cent and descent will be and in what conditions they will occur.

All this underscores the extreme importance of obtaining possible information about the road ahead from the local population and being very attentive to such information. As they say, a clever tongue will take you to Rome. The difficulty lies in the fact that it is mostly impossible to extract anything from the local population. Most peasants here have not been beyond neighboring villages in their entire lives or, at most, the county town. About few years ago in Szechuan, it turned out that the residents of one village did not know that Mao Tse-tung had long died (Mao died in 1976) - the local authorities simply forgot to inform them about it. All this is again due to the mountainous terrain, which isolates people and makes some areas particularly inaccessible and cut off from the "big land".

How many times we discovered that peasants do not know the area lying a couple of dozen miles from their native village, have no idea about, say, a ruined temple located liter- ally under their noses. It happened to us, asking about the distance to our destination, to hear in response: "Forty li"[8], after walking five miles, again hear: "Forty li", after another five miles, again: "Forty li". Often, the obstacle to understanding is also the numerous local dialects, so that sometimes it is simply impossible to understand what they are telling you (as is known, Chinese from different localities sometimes do not understand each other, and the differences between some Chinese dialects are more significant than, say, between English and French). I remember, when we began to doubt whether we were moving correctly towards Shentangbao, the two of us could not understand a word, even approximately, from the speech of a girl who came out of a fanza. On the map our goal was called Shentangbao, but later we learned that all the locals pronounce this word almost in the Spanish manner - Santa Bu.

That same night, in the village hospital where we stopped for the night (we did not immediately realize that it was a hospital), an old man, who was also the chief doctor, pouring himself vodka from a canister that smelt of fusel oil, and from time to time casually taking out his dentures to clean them and put them back in place, told us in quite decent Mandarin that Santa Bu was not far away and all the way downhill. And the next morning, indeed having rolled down several miles downhill, we found the pass blocking Santa Bu. I think it was called Horse Tail.

In fairness, it should be mentioned that once at night we stubbornly asked all passers-by where the village of Shezhuang was, and were very angry to see puzzled faces in response. But how we laughed later, realizing that we had simply misread the character on the map, and in fact, the village was called Duzhuang. That's when we understood the locals' bewilderment.

Well, and finally, how many times in response to a question about the road we received one single significant phrase: "Tsou bu dao", which means "You won't make it". Sometimes it was accompanied by a brief comment: "There is a mountain road there".

In what circumstances can you get such an answer, and what does it say? What to do in this case: turn back or continue to move forward?

The phrase "Tsou bu dao" can be heard before storming a peak or a difficult pass, searching for approaches to them. It says that the local resident does not believe that you, moreover a "foreign devil", are capable of climbing to the peak or overcoming the pass along the given route, or that for some psychological reasons he does not want you to do it, or both. In the eyes of a local resident, you are a "crazy white man", miraculously found in the vicinity of his village, who, for some incomprehensible reasons, most likely out of sheer madness, seeks to climb the mountain, and for some reason not the easiest way and method. At the same time, it is possible that the local resident himself has never been on this mountain.

So how should one treat the answer "Tsou bu dao"? It's now, typing these lines, that I pose this question. In the mountains, it never occurred to us - we simply continued to move forward. And what else, apart from righteous anger and the phrase beginning from "F..." can a true rider respond to such an answer?!

Nevertheless, it testifies to the fact that a difficult ascent lies ahead and should make one wary.

To date, only once did it happen that we turned back, heeding the advice of a local resident, and this advice was given to us without words, and we did not ask for it. This happened in warm May in the Long Men gorge.

This place is a narrow stone sack, width varying from 70 to 7 feet at different sections, clamped by high, sometimes over 300 feet, sheer cliffs, abundant with caves and overgrown with trees at the tops. On the stone-strewn - from pebbles to large boulders - bottom of the gorge runs a small mountain river with crystal clear water - apparently, it was it that over millions of years carved this path among the rocks.

At one point there is a rather high, about 30 feet, waterfall. Following the extremely winding riverbed, the gorge gradually rises up for many miles, up to river source at the top of the mountain, which, as we knew, represents an underground spring. The height of the mountain is not indicated on the map, but the difference in altitude is not so small - at least because the river is sometimes almost year-round in a frozen state, the water continues to flow only under a thick, somewhere 40 inches, layer of ice, covered with snow on top.

Long Men gorge is famous for the whimsical shapes of its rocks, so with the onset of warmth on weekends, "moral freaks" (i.e., tourists) are brought here by bus. They are taken up the gorge for about a mile, after which they return back and satisfied, with the thought "I have been to the Long Men gorge", leave for Beijing. We, however, got there by chance, returning from Mount Ling.

Having inspected thirty white stone totems at the entrance to the gorge (those were busts of policemen who died in this area at different times and under different circumstances - and God forbid you suddenly stumble upon such busts at night, in the dark), and successfully putting to sleep the vigilance of the old men from the neighboring village sitting as a watchman at the entrance, we penetrated into the gorge on steel steeds, which is not only prohibited by the "Rules of Conduct in the Gorge", printed on the back of entrance tickets, but simply not provided for. And indeed - I am sure, we were the first to move through the gorge on a bicycle. The "moral freaks" from the group just brought into the gorge stared at us with open mouths.

Moving through Long Men gorge on an ordinary, non- mountain bike is impossible. Shifting the chain to the smallest driving sprocket and the largest driven one, overcoming slippery scree gravel and crossing over boulders, sometimes fording the river, we stubbornly moved forward and upward. Soon the "moral freaks" were far below. Having reached the waterfall, we decided to swim in it and take a short rest.

And I need to tell you, reader, that our goal in the gorge was a cave of a certain saint, marked on the map. Therefore, we constantly looked for it, but so far, we had not found any- thing similar.

After the waterfall, something gradually began to change in the gorge - perhaps the space, squeezed between the rocks, became narrower, the gorge began to twist even more sharply and change directions abruptly, there was more vegetation, the relief went steeper upwards. There were more large stones, the air became damp, cool, heavily saturated with moisture, it became somehow darker. On one section about 150 feet long, the river turned into ice, and since the ice was covered with a layer of snow, we had to move carefully, fearing hidden holes or cracks underneath. Then the river disappeared altogether, hiding under the rocks. It became much harder to move forward, often we had to carry bicycles on ourselves, choosing between the stones where to put our foot. Our attention was drawn to some inscriptions on the rocks. Approaching, we read: "You are going to death". We did not pay much attention to the inscriptions.

Stopping for a breather, we suddenly heard the silence reigning in the gorge, which was not there below. Not a single sound - neither a drop of water, nor a breath of wind, in the strip of blue sky above between the rocks - not a single bird.

The silence was absolute, somehow stony and damp. It was the first to bring us a sense of some anxiety.

The situation was aggravated by the fact that we did not find any saint's cave. However, we knew from experience that if there is any shabby sight near their village, the locals are ready, for the sake of profit, to present it as almost Forbidden City. We remembered that we seemed to have passed something resembling a small hole in the rock. In that case, what is our goal? We had been climbing for half a day and, judging by the map, climbed quite far. Maybe reach the top of the mountain, look at the underground spring - the source of the river, and there will be another slope to descent?

And then, a couple of dozen feet away, we saw him. It was a local resident, about fifty years old, as it seemed to me, dressed in ordinary peasant clothes, but very worn, thin, if not to say, skinny. His face bore the stamp of some kind of foolishness, he seemed like the local village fool. The fool came to the gorge not by chance: on his shoulder, holding it with one hand, he carried a long, about ten feet, quite thick and heavy-looking snag, once a tree trunk. The fact that he walked for it, apparently, to the top of the mountain (there were no snags in the gorge), for many miles, was not surprising - there is a lack of fuel in the Chinese village and every piece of wood or coal is highly valued. We were surprised at how easily, given his physique, he carried it, already not the first mile and even through this gorge, where it is not easy to walk even without a snag. Even a strong man should have bent under the weight of the load, but the fool walked as if nothing had happened, choosing places between the stones and deftly maintaining balance - on his face I did not notice a drop of sweat.

And yet it was strange to meet a person here, far from housing - at least, we did not expect such a meeting in this remote part of the gorge. But here we almost caught up with the fool. At that moment he stopped and, without lowering the snag, addressed us. But not with words - it was a moan, like a mute makes when he very much wants and tries to say something. He accompanied his moaning with energetic gestures of his free hand. And we immediately understood him.

The fool told us, in a manner of speaking for a mute, that we must not, under any circumstances, proceed further up the gorge. Nodding at him, we continued on. But after a few dozen feet, we stopped and decided to turn back. Why? Hard to say. *Something* was prompting us. Turning our steel steeds around, we began to descend. Soon we caught up with the fool, who had already gone quite a distance. The path among the stones was so narrow that for some time we had to move behind him at a forcedly low speed. But then, at a ford across the river, a gap appeared, and, overtaking the fool, we rushed downwards.

The descent through the Long Men gorge is hard to forget. When we reached the beginning of the gorge and saw the "moral freaks" (tourists) peacefully examining the rocks below, we felt as though we had been transported from something dark and eerie to something sunny, mundane, and therefore comforting.

However, it was not half an hour before clouds gathered from somewhere, and we were caught in the heavy rain on the road. Escaping onto Highway No. 104, we took shelter in a roadside eatery, where we dried off and, as a precaution against catching a cold, each took a drink of Argothou[9], also consuming several pounds of meat. What dangers did we avoid then, and were they even real? Since we did not reach the end of the gorge, this remains a mystery. However, it might belong to those mysteries better left unsolved.

It is also necessary to mention that, apart from the unexpectedly emerging mountains and passes, for at least approximate planning of a journey, a true rider must consider two more circumstances: the time of year and possible changes in weather conditions. The stable, sharply continental climate of Northern China is not rich in surprises. Moreover, it is favorable for journeys on steel steeds - precipitation here is rare and insignificant, winters are mostly snowless. However, there is something here that causes constant cursing. These are the strong winds that blow mainly in winter and spring from the north, which, due to the dryness of the local soil, carry clouds of sand. In Mandarin, there is a special word for them – Fengsha. I remember one winter, the sand covered the sky so much that it turned yellow, and the sun, due to some optical phenomenon, turned blue. On such days, if you don't fancy sand crunching on your teeth, it's better not to leave the house without a mask on your face (a respirator or even a gas mask will also do).

The wind, when strong, is either a scourge or an ally - depending on the direction - for a cyclist. How much strength can it take away or save! A ride of some 30 miles along the Badaling road to the international shooting range near Beijing, where we were going to shoot various types of weapons in cold February, is remembered as one of the toughest - thanks to the strong northern wind that day blowing right in our faces (later, during shooting, it swayed the targets, making aiming difficult).

When the wind blows from behind, an inexperienced cyclist might not even understand why it suddenly became so easy to ride - because at high speed of the cyclist himself, such a wind is not felt. And yet, the wind is a double-edged sword: it hinders when moving forward and helps when returning (or vice versa). The cyclist's dream is for the wind to timely change directions and always blow from behind.

There is a golden season here, when there are no winds and the weather is just perfect - the beginning and middle of autumn. But for a true rider, this is of no significance, for he is ready for a journey at any time of the year. The time of year, however, leaves a certain imprint on the journey. Take, for example, our summer trip to Bai Hua mount, when along the way and in the foothills, we swam in mountain rivers and waterfalls, sunbathed and cooled off, lying on the grass, in the shade of trees (although persistent local kids did not let us enjoy this rest for long) - even though after climbing Bai Hua we temporarily turned into semi-handicapped persons, but still this journey had some kind of a resort character. Winter journeys, like the Datong and Wutai ones, are harsh. Progress in winter is faster, as there is little reason to stop, and sometimes stop is not even possible - after active movement, you start cooling down quickly. Therefore, in winter, in case of signs of fatigue, it is better not to stand still, but, as we say, "change the mode of motion" i. e. alternate cycling with walking segments of the route.

In conclusion, it can be said that in addition to the circumstances we have tried to briefly outline above, there are a dozen others that will disrupt any of your plans.

JOURNEY PARTS
AND THEIR FEATURES

Depending on the terrain traversed by a true rider on a steel steed or on foot, a journey can be divided into several parts. These are: 1/ Leaving the city limits, 2/ Traveling across flat terrain, 3/ Climbing uphill, 4/ Descending, 5)/Off road biking, 6/ Mountaineering, 7)/Entering a city, 8/ Stops for food and overnight. Let's delve into the characteristics of each of these parts.

1/ Leaving the city limits

We always set out early in the morning, sometimes at dawn. Exiting a city like Beijing takes about 1.5 hours. Since all thoughts are occupied with the upcoming multi-mile run and the mountains, the departure seems trivial. That's why, when setting out on a journey for the first time, we lost an extra couple of hours, getting lost in the network of roads on the western outskirts of Beijing. Since then, we carefully study the route of departure from the city on the map. And in general, during departure, you need to be on the alert, because at this time, as if to spite, something can happen.

If the departure coincides with rush hours - 7-8 a.m., when millions of Beijing residents joyfully rush to work, you have to move in a dense stream of cyclists. In some places you can even get stuck in a bike traffic jam, which will waste a lot of your time. Almost always, there is a couple of "racers" who can't stand seeing some "foreign devils" riding faster than everyone. It never occurs to the "racers" that unlike them, we have hundreds of miles ahead of us and that we are riding at a normal cruising speed. Needless to say, not once has any of the "racers" managed to overtake us. We always took such races as an opportunity to warm up and fully wake up. However, once we encountered a worthy competitor in a short distance, who made us sweat: he rode on the road to the Beijing Shou Gang Steel plant for several miles up to the entrance, where he disappeared, lagging behind us by only a dozen feet (perhaps he was the factory's physical education teacher).

When we finally leave the city, we traditionally make a short stop. Pleased, we look at it, dusty, smoky, noisy, from the outside.

2/ Traveling across flat terrain

After leaving the city, the journey across flat terrain be- gins, which can take up to 50%, sometimes more, of the time on the journey. Let's clarify again that truly flat terrain is extremely rare in mountainous regions, even in valleys lying between mountains. Therefore, by flat terrain, we mean such where the angle of ascent allows you to move on it by bicycle for a long time. The angle of ascent can sometimes be very insignificant, so that an inexperienced cyclist doesn't even feel it, but this doesn't mean that such an ascent doesn't take additional strength from the cyclist.

In our first Datong journey on its first day, we mainly moved across completely flat terrain, as it seemed to us then. The freshness and vigor of the first day's strength often mask the slight changes in the road's angle of inclination. A week later, having covered 600 miles by that time, we returned along the same road and were surprised at how easy it was for us - because the road constantly went down at a very small angle.

We were even more surprised by how we climbed uphill all the first day and didn't notice it. Thus, a very gentle ascent can be well felt by contrast with a descent or a truly flat section, as well as in a state of sufficient fatigue.

Beijing is located at the northern tip of the Huabei Plain. To the north and west, it is closely embraced by the northern spurs of the Taihang range, further to the north lie the southern spurs of the

Greater Khingan range and the Inner Mongolian Highlands, to the west - the Huangtu Highlands, including several mountain systems.

The paths leading to the highest mountains, to the most beautiful places, go from Beijing to the west and southwest - it is precisely there that a true rider heads. Therefore, in the first part of the journey, the true rider continuously ascends higher and higher above sea level, returning back - descends.

Traveling across flat terrain in a journey has as little in common with sports cycling as mountaineering does with sports rock climbing. In rock climbing, an athlete strives to climb a certain predetermined rock chosen for the competition as quickly as possible, showing the best time. Naturally, he fully exerts himself in this. In mountaineering, however, the serious ascent lasts for days and sometimes weeks, may include not one rock wall, and the route is often known only from the climbing map. A mountaineer cannot exert himself; on the contrary, he constantly saves energy on any, even the slightest movement, to always have some reserve of it. Similarly, in cycling sports, the task is to cover a predetermined distance in the shortest possible time. In a journey, however, a rider has many hundreds, sometimes a thousand miles of road with unknown conditions ahead, so, like a mountaineer, he has to carefully conserve his strength.

Moreover, we usually use a method in a journey to save energy, unknown and unthinkable for a sports cyclist: using passing transport for movement. Fortunately, in China, there is one type of transport extremely suitable for this purpose - mini-tractors with cargo trailers, abundantly used in the local village. The technique of using tractors is very simple: when one overtakes you, you need to grab onto it with your hand without delay. Their speed, 20-25 mph, is just perfect for such a maneuver. Stern drivers in huge sun-protective glasses, worn against dust, or sometimes passengers in the trailer, almost always, with rare exceptions, do not object to some two devils hanging onto their tractor, moreover, if they are going to turn off the road, they give a hand signal. Moreover, peasants themselves sometimes use this method of movement. You with your partner can grab onto a tractor from the right and left or together from one side. You just need to pay attention to the road conditions and make sure not to hook any protruding part of the trailer with the bicycle's "horn" (as happened to Victor on the way from Guanglin to Yuxian, which led to his fall).

Oh, tractors! We recognize the distinctive sound of their engines from several miles away, determining the brand of the tractor, be it a heavily stone-laden Orient Wind-30 or a nimble blue Tremendous Force, which, if it goes empty, is almost impossible to grab onto. How many of our efforts have they saved on the roads of the Celestial Empire! Sometimes, a tractor pulled us a good ten miles. However, tractors are not always so frequently encountered, and in relatively remote places, they are completely absent - you dream of a tractor, wait hopefully to hear the familiar sounds from afar - and not a single one all day. With hundreds and thousands of miles traveled, the reflex to grab any convenient tractor becomes so ingrained that even later, in Beijing, hearing the sudden familiar rattling (tractors very rarely, but sometimes wander into the city, to its outskirts) you catch yourself with the same thought. But to be honest, at the very beginning of our journeys, it seemed to me that grabbing onto a tractor was something unsporty, diminishing the value of overcoming the path by one's own efforts. But such idealistic views had to be abandoned very quickly.

On the way across flat terrain, besides tractors, a rider has another frequent companion, but unlike tractors, an un- wanted one (with rare exceptions), which is – lamèidì. What is that? Once, a professor of Chinese ethnography in our university filled our heads with stories about shuoshudì[10]. Since then, on the roads of the Celestial Empire, we only met one shuoshudì, but we encountered hundreds, thousands of lamèidì, about which no one warned us.

The thing is, there is a lot of coal in China - I write this not by hearsay, but having experienced it literally on my own skin. From the official statistics of the PRC, it is also known that China is provided with underground coal reserves for 1,000 years (these are only the explored reserves). Absolutely most of the electricity here is generated by burning coal, and it is also used to heat all cities and the entire village north of the Yangtze River in winter (south of the Yangtze, heating does not exist). Huge coal piles in the courtyards of boiler rooms, daily scurrying cycle rickshaws, heavily loaded with pressed coal briquettes, coal dust in the air, on houses, cars, on your clothes, in your lungs - without all this, a Beijing winter is unthinkable.

So where does the coal come from in Beijing? To the west (exactly in that direction where a true rider heads), several hundred miles from the capital, lies Shanxi Province, which is called China's coal base. It is from there that the "black gold"[11] (which we called nothing else but "black shit") constantly trickles into Beijing. But by autumn, the trickles become more and more numerous, and by winter they turn into one gigantic river of coal. This river consists of coal trains and lamèidì. The word lamèidì literally translates as "dragging coal." In Chinese driver slang, "to drag, to pull" means "to transport," and is also used by taxi drivers in relation to passengers.

So lamèidì is a cargo truck, usually Oriental Wind or Liberation, with raised sides, necessarily with a trailer, loaded with coal in a heap, almost to the impossible limit (on top, the coal, so that it does not spill out, is covered with some torn film, which is tied to the body - and don't think that the coal does not spill out at that). Why is the lamèidì so heavily loaded? Because lamèidì (this name applies not only to coal trucks, but also to their drivers) has his personal interest in it, the truck is mainly rented. Therefore, the lamèidì rushes along the roads at a frantic speed, often crashing or overturning in the process (we saw several fresh accidents with our own eyes) and there are no weekends for it. In the cabin, there are 2-3 drivers who take turns replacing each other, and the lamèidì is on the road day and night. Thus, the lamèidì shuttles back and forth between Shanxi and Beijing all winter, all year. The number of lamèidì is enormous. The concentration of them on different roads varies, but even one of them, when you meet it, deafens with iron clatter and an obligatory horn, and covers with a cloud of coal dust. What about coal routes, where lamèidì move in endless columns?

I remember, on a narrow road with deep ditches from Yuxian to Xiheying, two lamèidì collided, and all traffic stopped. So, we rode past a column of trucks for about an hour until we reached the scene of the accident, from where another column stretched in the opposite direction.

We ended up on a coal route (certainly not by choice - simply unaware that it passed there) on the section from Yangyuan to Datong in December 199... The journey on it was a significant physical and psychological test. Arriving in Datong and having washed up our faces with soap with difficulty, we discovered that our eyelashes still remained as if coquettishly outlined in black, as though we were regulars at the Kunlun[12]. After combing our hair (or rather, struggling to untangle the tangles), we had to wash our hands again. (Generally, in a long, harsh bike tour, when grooming yourself in the morning, you should always comb your hair first, and only then wash your hands with soap). Victor, who wore glasses, still had two black spots on his nose even a month after the Datong trip ended - that's how ingrained the coal dust was in the skin. I'm not even mentioning that the clatter of iron and deafening sharp honks lingered in our ears for a long time.

For peasants, through whose villages the coal route passes, it brings considerable profit - they collect pieces of coal that fall from the trucks and sweep the coal dust into bags - we have witnessed this spectacle more than once. Much greater profit is had by the eateries and drivers' lodges located on the route and especially at coal loading points.

Since then, having scouted all the roads west of Beijing, we carefully avoid coal routes. However, encounters with in- dividual lamèidì on flat terrain, especially in winter, are unavoidable. Here is where I must say that we had a couple of instances where lamèidì showed themselves in a completely different light.

When we, having overcome the difficult Sea Buckthorn climb, descended into Taipingbao, and then moved through the sandy hills further west, on one of the ascents we were overtaken by a large 10-ton empty truck (I remember, it was a Nissan), which suddenly stopped next to us. Paying no attention to this, we continued walking uphill. However, the truck began to slowly drive alongside us, then a head appeared from the window, offering a lift (where, was not a question, as there was only one road ahead for the next 40 miles). "How much?" - we asked. "No money needed," was the reply, after which our steel steeds found themselves in the coal-dusty body of the truck, and we - in the cabin.

I must say, the cabin of the Nissan turned out to be so spacious that we almost effortlessly fit in it along with the three lamèidì - as it turned out, one of them, the craftier one, rented the truck, the other two were hired as helpers. That's how we got to know lamèidì better and learned a lot about their life and hard earnings over the 40 miles journey. However, there is no need to go into detail here, except to mention the "yellow pussies".

As we chatted, we discovered that all lamèidì conversation topics gradually boiled down to one, apparently, the main and most important during the long hours they spent in the cabin - about women. After all, lamèidì in their detachment from women are like sailors setting off on a long voyage. Female forms even appeared to them in the relief of the mountains passing by the cabin window. And what kind of suitor is a dirty, grimy lamèidì? Even if he washed up (which is unlikely), where would he find the time for romances? Therefore, conversations about women for lamèidì meant conversations about "yellow pussies"[13]. Especially one of them, a young guy with completely rotten teeth, knew the road well in this respect - it was felt that he had been traveling this route for a long time. Sometimes, when we passed some lodge, he noted that there were "yellow pussies" there, naming the price (extraordinarily low, by the way). We were also thoroughly questioned about "yellow pussies" in our homeland.

Thus, passing the time, we arrived in the darkness at our destination, which turned out to be the same for both of us - the small county town of Yuxian, which, among other things, houses one of the coal loading points. Subsequently, something happened to us there, which will be discussed later. The caring lamèidì not only drove us to the place but also helped us stay overnight in a cheap drivers' lodge, for all this we retained the warmest memories of them.

The second case, which turned into a test of our nerves' strength, occurred almost in the same place but a few days later, when we were returning back. To get to Beijing on time, we had to cross the Kongjian Pass that evening, after which we planned to spend the night at Dage's. But try as we might, by around 11 p.m. we only reached the beginning of the pass, where the village of Kongjian is located. Entering the last still open eatery there to warm up (it was December) and have a snack, we also discussed our further actions.

There wasn't much to discuss, really. Crossing the Kongjian Pass on foot at night, with its sheer cliffs and leopards, was very risky, and we had almost reconciled to spending the night not at Dage's, but in this remote village, and returning to Beijing a day later.

But then, in the pitch darkness outside the eatery's window, beams of light appeared, then a sound, and within a minute a truck that had descended from the Sea Buckthorn climb was already braking at its doors. The doors opened, and three men entered the eatery, at the sight of whom there was no doubt about who they were. The three sat down at the next table, ordered two bottles of Argothou, some snacks, and, drinking and eating, began discussing their affairs. However, only two of them drank, while the third abstained.

From this, we concluded that the three were not planning to stay overnight in Kongjian, but would continue their journey - the abstainer was apparently driving on this stretch of the road. Soon, snippets of their conversations reaching us confirmed the accuracy of our conclusion. Then I went outside and inspected the vehicle. It was an ordinary Oriental Wind, whose cabin barely accommodates three people, but the body, to my satisfaction, was empty.

And so, when the bottles at the next table were empty, the guests paid the hostess and were about to leave, we respectfully greeted them and asked for a lift over the pass. Having inquired whether we would freeze in the body, the three immediately agreed. I positioned myself on the right side of the truck's body, Victor on the left, and we placed the bicycles close to the cabin. We no longer paid any attention to the thick layer of coal dust covering the floor and sides of the body.

Then something happened that we did not expect: not the abstainer, but on the contrary, the most drunk, with a red face, very excited after a bottle and a half of 56% Argothou, got behind the wheel. We remembered how many lamèidì constantly crashed on flat highways - and we had at least 3000 feet pass serpentine unpaved road ahead, a dirt, rocky road, where in places two cars couldn't pass each other, with sheer cliffs on one side and drops of several hundred feet on the other. But it was too late to get out at that moment when we had already started!

The Red-faced drove the truck like a madman. It was clear that if the truck, failing to navigate another turn of the serpentine road, plunged down, you wouldn't have time to do anything. The thought came to mind: do leopards feed on carrion? A couple of times, in narrow places, I looked over the side down and couldn't make out the road - right at the wheel, the abyss began. Another time we almost hit a large stone, suddenly appearing on the road (apparently, there was a rockfall in that place), but the Red-faced managed to brake sharply and bypass it - fortunately, the road was wide enough there. However, we didn't experience any fear - just a clear awareness that we had a chance to fall into the abyss.

When the truck passed the highest point of the pass and the paved road began, we realized that, apparently, we would make it. Another half hour later, having thanked the lamèidì, we unloaded our steel steeds right opposite Dage's inn. That's how the lamèidì helped us for the second time.

Besides tractors and lamèidì, on the road, a rider sometimes encounters other vehicles, including horses and donkeys. However, they no longer have special significance for our story.

Traveling on flat terrain, if it is long enough, becomes monotonous, and then - difficult. The most challenging for us, as I recall, was overcoming the final stretch to Datong on our first trip. On that frosty December day, we covered only about 90 miles from Yuxian – Xiheying – Huaxiaoying – Yangyuan – Datong along a road that steadily inclined upward at a slight angle. Already on the Xiheying-Huaxiaoying stretch, we began implementing a method of three miles runs followed by rest (something we never do in normal conditions). However, after Huaxiaoying, upon entering the aforementioned coal route, we had to, falling short of Datong by only 10-12 miles and already in the dark, use a passing vehicle (we resorted to this only three times during all our trips). This time it wasn't a lamèidì, since they were all going in loaded condition, but a small minibus - and there, its driver charged us amply for the ride.

In the same first trip, there was a very easy, even some- what magical, road on flat terrain: from Datong to the village of Gu Ding Qiao. First, this road crossed a wide steppe and was truly flat. Second, it had almost no traffic. Third, it suddenly warmed up. We achieved our goal - we covered 350 miles, reached the famous Yungang Caves and saw them with our own eyes (now you can't deceive us with tales about these caves), rested in Datong, and, content, set off back in the evening, intending to spend the night in some village. For this occasion, we even bought two bottles of excellent "Blue Ribbon" beer in Datong city, but drank it as darkness fell, in silence, in the vast steppe. How wonderful and easy it was to ride after that! And the 22 miles to the village flew by almost unnoticed.

3/ Climbing uphill

Analogous to point 2), by climb we mean a stretch of road rising uphill at such an angle that it has to be overcome on foot. Let me tell you, a true rider always prefers to move on a steel steed, dismounting only in the most extreme cases. On a mountain bike, it's possible to conquer very steep climbs, however, if the climb, even not very steep, is prolonged, it is overcome on foot, in the interest of conserving energy. To save physical and mental energy, the right attitude towards the climb is crucial.

When you face a pass, the most important things are: first, remember that the climb can be long, say, 30 miles, and second, never forget that no matter how long it lasts, it will surely end. One should not hope for the best and at the same time not fall into pessimism. Comfort yourself with the thought of how exhilarating it will be to roll down from the pass after completing the climb, especially keeping in mind that the longer the climb, the longer the descent will be. If after an ascent of many miles you find a 300-feet descent, think about how easy your return journey will be on this road. In general, ascents, like nothing else, teach one not to cherish hopes, to be cautious about seemingly beautiful prospects, and overall, develop a philosophical calm. How many times, dripping with streams of sweat in summer, bending under the icy wind that intensifies with altitude in winter, pushing steel steeds uphill for miles (and sometimes carrying them), we hoped that beyond this bend of the road, beyond that rock, a wide panorama of mountains (or a tunnel) would finally open up, signaling the proximity of the highest point of the pass, and then that point itself would finally be under our feet. And how many times behind those bends and rocks were just another bend and another rock, or, worse, a mountain arose so immense that the hope cherished few minutes ago became laughably naive. But how many times can one hope in vain? We became skeptical and did not believe even the most obvious signs of the end of the ascent until the very end - it was like a protective reaction of the psyche. Eventually, a certain calmness developed, where mental energy was no longer wasted in vain on expecting anything, good or bad, from the next turn in the road; hopes for a quick end to the climb no longer arose, we simply kept in mind that it, no matter how long, would eventually end, reaching the coveted highest point no longer caused wild joy but was perceived as something due. Thus, the climb teaches calmness and patience.

Moreover, it is on the climb (and not the descent), especially a steep one, exacerbated by physical and psychological fatigue, that one may experience a distinctive feeling of being lost in the mountains, a sense of one's insignificance in the face of huge mountains and, more broadly, in the face of nature. In such extreme moments, a person may suddenly see some aspects of their past life (i.e., before this climb) differently, a reassessment of certain values may occur in their soul. Such changes in the psyche can be more or less stable.

I remember very well how on one of the first passes, I had a feeling of the futility, excessiveness, and therefore, the unnecessity of engaging in any martial arts, to which I had dedicated quite a lot of time over ten years. Victor, on a pass in the Wutai Mountains, suddenly talked about how we did not treat our women well enough.

It will be easier on the ascent if you properly establish your relationship with the mountains in advance: a person and mountains are parts of one indivisible whole, called nature, with no relationship of one dominating the other. It's ludicrous to talk about "conquering" a mountain, millions of years old, by a person climbing it. On the other hand, leopards living in the mountains apparently don't feel any sense of lostness or insignificance before the mountains, so why should a human feel it?

In climbing, the guiding principle is akin to that for traversing flat terrain: progress swiftly, pausing solely as re- quired, while conserving energy by means of efficient motion and varying body postures. A fortuitous tractor on the ascent is a great luck (if a suitable road exists), moreover, on a steep enough ascent, you can even catch a heavily loaded and therefore slowly climbing lamèidì. However, such luck is very rare, and almost always on an ascent, you must rely solely on your own strength. And sometimes, they seem to be on the verge of running out. One of the most challenging ascents we experienced was from the turn at Shijiazhuang to the area of Fighting Fish village in February 19... We overcame it by 11 p.m., having covered 25 miles mostly in darkness.

4/ Descending

After overcoming the ascent, a rider, by the laws of nature, faces a descent. How to convey what this is? Let's try to explain it, at least approximately. Descending on a steel steed is something directly opposite to the just-completed ascent - it requires no physical or psychological effort, except that some strain falls on the hands holding the handlebars and pressing the brake levers, and sometimes in winter, the face is scorched by a stream of oncoming air. You've endured a lot, climbing for long hours to the highest point of the pass. All this time your gaze was fixed on ever-new rocks and ridges, blocking your horizon - you walked as if in the tight embrace of the mountains. You've had many thoughts, as the ascent, occupying your body, leaves your mind free, and eventually, there's no energy left for conversation. The struggle with physical and mental fatigue has left its mark on your thoughts.

And suddenly everything changes instantly: beyond the next rock over the road, between the enclosing rocks, a gap of clear blue sky suddenly opens. With every step, it expands more and more, and now a vast panorama of the mountain landscape unfolds before you - you are at the highest point of the pass. Sometimes this swift transition is preceded by a black echoing tunnel, where, blinded by the contrast of darkness and bright white light at its end, you lose your sense of space for a moment. Now the landscape will continuously and rapidly change with your movement, with new views opening at every turn, from harsh mountain ridges and rocks to valleys and fields below - all unfolding before you at wind speed as you literally plummet from a height of 3,000-6,000 feet.

You no longer need to walk, pushing the steel steed for miles - you sit on it, then gain maximum speed within a few dozen feet, and no longer pedal. From this moment, nothing but the descent remains in your head - as if the powerful oncoming airstream instantly blows all thoughts out of your head. The descent brings oblivion and self-forgetfulness, lasting quite a while (in this sense, the descent is a form of meditation). Besides, it gives a very peculiar, incomparable, vivid joy (which you then want to experience again and again), brought by a feeling close to free falling (and therefore never experienced when descending a mountain by car or motorcycle - tested).

If the slope's steepness reaches 30 degrees, the descent occurs at very high speed. And as you understand, a true rider presses the brake levers only when absolutely necessary, i.e., only at sharp turns, abundant in mountain serpentine road - the very top of the pass. The road and rocks flash by at breakneck speed, even a perfectly tuned mountain bike, even on paved road, begins to vibrate slightly from the speed, the vibration transferring to the rider's body. Imagine if the descent is on a gravel road, always stony in the mountains - in this case, the vibration is greatly intensified, and constant jolts from wheel impacts on stones add to it. If nuts are not tightened enough on the bike, they will gradually unwind, and it's easy to understand what this can lead to at speeds of 25-40 mph. Thus, a serious descent requires complete confidence in the condition of the steel steed.

Such a descent also requires full concentration on it. If, for example, a stone or a hidden pit lies 150 feet ahead on your path, you will reach it in 3-5 seconds, and God forbid you get distracted from the road during these seconds. An unexpected collision with even a minor obstacle at high speeds can result in a fall, the consequences of which are unpredictable. When passing a steep turn of the serpentine road at the highest possible speed, you also need to precisely calculate the speed and angle of inclination to the surface - at this moment, it's as if you and the bicycle become one entity. In the upper, most steep and winding part of the descent, you can only glance away from the road for a second, mainly noting the changing landscape with peripheral vision. Only in the middle part of the descent, where the serpentine road turns into more extended straight sections with smoother turns, do you catch your breath and see where you have ended up. However, since the steepest part still remains in the middle, and there is often no need to brake strongly, this is where you reach the highest, dizzying speed. When you experience this for the first time, it's not easy to maintain such speed and not give in to the urge to brake - indeed: it seems incredible for a bicycle, and the thought may occur - will the bicycle withstand it? These straight sections have their own charm, somewhat different from passing through the serpentine road. I especially remember the straight descent before Guangling. Here it should be noted that a true rider considers it an honor to pass the descent using brakes as infrequently as possible.

In the lower part of the descent, the steepness de- creases, the road becomes even straighter, but a sufficiently high speed is still maintained. It's amusing if an encircling village happens to be on the way here: local elders often sit on the side, basking in the sun. They don't even have time to understand what happened when we flash by. If any local resident manages to spot the fleeting devils, they usually just freeze in amazement. Only once did a villager cry out in surprise at the sight of us: "Oh - oh - oh!" The spectacle of rapidly passing "foreign devils" through their native village could indeed astonish even Li Kui[14]. A minute - and the village is behind. It should only be added that when moving through a village, one should be careful not to run into playing children on the road.

In the descent's final segment, the road gradually levels out, reducing our speed and diminishing the intense sensations. Now you can simply relax, lean on the handlebars, and without thinking about anything, while admiring the surroundings where you descended from the mountains, indulge in a smooth motion downwards, until the wheels finally come to a stop at the end of the descent. Stony mountain descents, lacking asphalt covering, differ slightly from the above description: here, brakes must be used very often, and the speed is somewhat reduced. However, the lack of speed is amply compensated by slaloming between stones and pits. On a stony descent, you can't take your eyes off the road for a second, even in the lower, more gradual part. Sometimes the conditions of a stony descent become close or in some sections turn into off road biking, which will be discussed below. Such was the descent from Mount Ling.

We have tried to convey the very strong sensations of a high-speed descent, which perhaps constitute a significant part of the quintessence and meaning of a mountain bike tour. But there are also descents of a different nature: relatively gradual and usually very long (they usually follow the same gradual and long ascents, or extensive areas of "flat" terrain, which in reality are constantly slightly increasing). On such a descent, usually with asphalt covering, you roll down calmly, at medium or even low speed, concentration on the road is not required, so you can observe the surroundings. However, even such a descent, not being an extreme situation but mesmerizing with its constant free movement, not requiring the slightest physical effort, is another type of meditation and is still so attractive that it is worth overcoming hundreds of miles for these 30 - 40 minutes. The most memorable gradual descent for me starts a few miles from Laiyuan city and stretches all the way to the police post on the border of Hebei and Shanxi provinces. It is so prolonged that there I first thought that it would be good to install an additional longitudinal handlebar, covered with foam, allowing you to lie on it with your hands and place your back almost horizontally (until then, I considered such handlebars to be a show-off). On this descent, free from cars, warmed by the sun, you could even occasionally close your eyes for a short time and almost sleep.

In conclusion, about night descents. One might ask: why descend at night? As we have already said, starting an as- cent, you cannot know when it will end, and it may well happen (and does happen) that you find yourself at the highest point of the pass already in the dark. Even if you start the ascent at 2 p.m., it does not guarantee that it will not end at midnight. Since there are no villages or any accommodation at the top of the pass, you have to roll down at night to find somewhere to spend the night. Why not go down on foot? Firstly, a true rider would consider it a disgrace, secondly, this way you might not reach a village by morning.

Perhaps we should have long ago installed removable flashlights on our bikes, but for various reasons, we never did this over the years. Therefore, at night you roll down at your own risk, at a slightly reduced speed, braking when the bicycle accelerates too much. Orientation in the dark is facilitated under the following conditions: a) if the moon shines in the sky, b) if there are white lines on the edges of a paved road, c) if the road passes through a more or less wide area, illuminated if not by the moon, then by the stars, d) if the road is bordered by trees that can be distinguished from the darkness, e) if villages are encountered on the sides of the road, even at a distance. If, however, it is a moonless night and the road goes somewhere between rocks or mountain ridges, orientation becomes much more difficult. In any case, rolling down at night requires constant tense peering ahead.

There is also something in it - rolling down into complete darkness towards the unknown. At the same time, you involuntarily tense up, expecting that you will soon encounter some obstacle or run over some unevenness on the road. However, only once, during the Wutai Mountain trip, on a night descent after the village of Chuanling, did this really happen: a fist-sized stone got under my wheel. After ten feet of free flight in the dark, I safely landed on the road, completely unharmed, as was my Wild Cat. For this reason, during a night descent, one should not ride too close to each other, especially directly behind a companion, because then No. 2 will run over the fallen first. This rule, however, also applies to daytime descents, on which we usually maintain a distance of at least 50 yards. In general, for a night descent, it is recommended to pay maximum attention, reduce speed, and occasionally give sound signals, especially if there are villages nearby.

5/ Off-road biking

What do we mean by off-road biking in relation to biking conditions in China? It is very simple - this is a descent (rarely - an ascent) in mountainous terrain, in off-road conditions, on a rocky slope, a gorge, along the bed of a mountain river, when stones and pits become so numerous that it becomes impossible to bypass them, and you have to move directly over them, and so large that you have to significantly reduce speed and switch to the lowest gear ratios of rotational torque from the driving to the driven sprocket.

Off road biking is the pinnacle of mountain biking, for such terrain is impossible to traverse on a regular bike, and the most challenging off-road terrains cannot be conquered even with an off-road jeep or motorcycle, except perhaps for a specially adapted off-road sports motorcycle (though a motorcycle cannot be carried over sections that are only passable on foot).

Depending on the level of difficulty, we categorize off- road biking into several types. The complexity depends on the size of the predominant stones and the depth of the pits, as well as the presence or absence of mountain rivers. Let's illustrate this with a couple of examples.

The southern descent from Mount Ling, in its middle and lower parts, represents an off-road biking of medium difficulty: descent there requires frequent braking at reduced speed, constant maneuvering to avoid overly sharp stones and deep pits, yet still moving over large stones covering the road, through dips and trenches, sometimes sliding on gravel piles, etc. The cyclist experiences intense shaking, forcing a firm grip on the handlebars and strong pressure on the pedals, the whole body tensed, sometimes needing to stand in the saddle to absorb shocks. Stones fly in all directions from under the wheels, some shooting out with great force, and if it has rained, mud flies too. Off-road biking is similar to a regular descent in that it fully captures the cyclist's attention, but unlike a descent, it represents a significant physical challenge: after a good off-road session, the arms (especially wrists and forearms), back, and thighs ache.

The Long Men Gorge is a classic example of the highest difficulty off-road biking, and on most of its sections, due to the small angle of the terrain, biking is possible both downhill and uphill. Here, you move at speeds no more than 3-5 mph, shifted to the lowest gear (otherwise, movement is impossible), constantly, often with great effort, pedaling. The cyclist continuously overcomes very large rocks and boulders, rising 10-15 inches from the surface, riding over them, climbing onto stone ledges and descending, sometimes getting stuck in deep, viscous sand, and suddenly fording a fast mountain river up to half a meter deep - all requiring constant and considerable physical effort, just to stay in the saddle, let alone cross a boulder the size of an arm span. Moreover, since crossing such terrain is possible only at very low speeds, constant balancing and maintaining equilibrium is necessary, losing which could result in a fall onto sharp rocks. The cyclist in the Long Men Gorge literally scrambles over rocks. An inexperienced person would not believe that such terrain is passable on a bike.

The main thrill of off-road biking lies in traversing the most rugged and rocky terrain at the highest possible speed. Although we never deliberately sought out such terrain, gorges and rocky descents naturally appeared before us.

6/ Mountaineering

If off-road biking is the pinnacle of mountain biking, then mountaineering, in most cases, is the peak of the entire journey, as its primary goal is often the summit of a particular mountain.

Why do we strive for the mountains? First, because the only thing better than mountains are the mountains that one has not yet visited. As is known, a true rider requires various challenges from time to time, without which life would be bland and boring (here we come very close to the very philosophy of mountain biking). Mountains represent a special challenge for the body and spirit, which, if one does not cross a certain line (!), does not pose a risk to life and is even beneficial to health: mountain air, nature, and solitude have the most beneficial effect on a person. The process of ascent and reaching the summit provide unforgettable and unique sensations and feelings, as no two mountains are the same.

There are those who believe the saying "A wise man circumvents the mountain rather than climbing it" is true. However, a mountain never rises alone on flat terrain; mountains always stretch in chains for hundreds and thousands of miles, grouping into massifs. Going around a mountain is often impossible, or it would require a gigantic detour. If a person in a mountainous area were to follow such a saying, they would be doomed to sit in one place all their life and never see what lies beyond the nearby pass.

If the ancient Chinese had followed this adage, China would occupy an area smaller than, say, Washington state in the US. It should be noted that such a saying could only have originated in a country with flat terrain; a Tibetan, born and living all his life in the highlands, would consider this statement the ravings of a madman.

In general, a person espousing the saying "A wise man will not go up the mountain..." should be cautioned against voicing their views aloud near a company of mountaineers, especially if they have ice axes with them. True riders simply tie up such a person and hand them over to miners (we will talk about miners below).

Furthermore, ascetics and monks in various countries always sought to escape from the hustle and bustle of the world to the mountains, if only they were around, and China is no exception. Over time, many mountains, where renowned teachers lived and taught, were surrounded by an aura of sanctity, and over the centuries, numerous temples and monasteries grew on them. Some mountains were also pilgrimage sites for Chinese emperors. The most famous mountains are the highest, although in China there is also the saying: "The name of a mountain is not in its height, but in its sanctity." If a village has a couple of hills nearby, local peasants, seeking to attract passing travelers for profit, paint this saying on the walls of their houses.

Besides followers of teachings and religions, mountains have always attracted warriors (I mean warriors in spirit): first, they too always sought secluded places; second, training in the mountains allows achieving enhanced results, both psychologically and physically. This is confirmed by modern research data, explained by the influence of the mountain climate, mainly the purity of the air, its thinness, and reduced atmospheric pressure. Athletes from control groups who trained in mountain camps invariably showed better results and increased endurance compared to groups that trained in ordinary flat conditions. The names of many schools of traditional Chinese wushu feature various mountains.

It should also be added that due to their inaccessibility, especially for those unfamiliar with the paths, mountains in China (and not only) have historically served as refuges for bandits. They set up their camps there, from which they made raids, terrorizing the local population, and if they were strong enough, established their own orders in the area. In China, such people are called "tufei", which simply means "local bandits." Coming to power in the country, the communists in China waged a broad campaign against the tufei entrenched in the mountains, as they often posed a threat to their dictatorship in the regions, especially in remote mountain areas, where tufei often represented the real power. It must be said that by that time (early 1950s), due to the prolonged turmoil in the country caused by wars, anti-Japanese and civil, the tufei had gained significant strength. It is difficult to fight in the mountains, especially in a country where they occupy a large part of the territory, and the government's fight against the tufei stretched over decades. Nevertheless, the tufei have not disappeared completely and still exist in China today (about our encounter with the tufei from Mount Bai Hua, see below).

As you understand, it was not the prospect of encountering tufei that drew us to the mountains, but rather the Buddhist and Daoist temples, the glorious traditions of spiritual seekers and martial arts masters. More accurately, the remnants of these traditions, since they are suppressed or simply forgotten in modern China. A classic expedition can be described as one aimed at reaching a mountain, visiting a temple or monastery there, and ascending its peak (though, of course, not every one of our trips was classic).

We don't wear heavy mountain boots or rock-climbing shoes, and we don't carry a set of hooks and anchors to hammer into rock crevices. Our only rope is used solely for tying backpacks to the bike rack. We don't spend nights hanging on a cliff face or heating up canned food on a stove placed between our knees. Thus, we markedly differ from mountaineers. All our ascents took place in the mid-mountain range, i.e., at altitudes up to 12,000 feet (high mountain ranges start higher), and along routes that didn't require climbing gear (though a couple of times we came very close to that line). Nevertheless, to distinguish this part of our journey, which strictly speaking is called mountain tourism, we refer to it as mountaineering.

Like high-altitude mountaineering, the key here is choosing the right route. Multiple routes, each with its own level of difficulty, lead to a single peak; an ascent to 10,000 feet may be tougher than another to 15,000. Typically, on every mountain explored by people, especially in China, there is one easiest route, sometimes even a road, albeit a rocky one, leading to the summit. Ascending this road can be done with bikes and requires only patience. The trick, however, is that this road is not marked on maps and can be hard to find in some cases.

True riders, seeking to challenge themselves, sometimes undertake ascents along the most difficult routes, where only animal trails exist, or, for instance, in cliffs where no one goes. In such cases, the steel steeds have to be left in a secure place below.

The hardest part is visually identifying the goal of the ascent - the peak - without a map of the mountains. This is quite challenging, as from below, it's impossible to discern the few hundred feet difference in height between several nearby peaks, and the direction must be chosen from the bottom. Mistakes lead to lengthy detours. As you ascend, the panorama of the surrounding landscape constantly changes, as the viewpoint shifts, and what seemed an unattainable peak becomes just another ridge. Constant and careful observation of the changing landscape is essential, with immediate adjustments to the direction as needed. The main role here belongs to the eye. Additionally, comparing several peaks, one should look for anything distinguishing one, like artificial objects - a marker, antennas, or masts. Such a peak is most likely the true summit. Sometimes meteorologists nest there or radio beacons are placed for aviation.

It's more convenient to ascend following the terrain, for instance, along a mountain riverbed, or along the direction of ridges, avoiding cliffs. One should not move along the bottom of ravines or between ridges - while it may initially seem convenient, eventually, you'll have to climb out, and the further you go, the harder it gets. Seeking to shorten the path, extremes should be avoided. Once, in our effort to reach the summit by the shortest route, we ended up on an almost vertical cliff. We progressed through its crevice, where over the centuries, grass and small bushes had grown in accumulated soil. The crevice gradually narrowed and disappeared. I was leading, with Victor below. Thankfully, we realized in time that climbing further without hooks and safety equipment was extremely risky, and after carefully descending, we went around the cliff.

During ascents, it's very important to conserve energy. You can never tell how much will be spent reaching the summit and descending, as the conditions of the ascent always remain somewhat unknown, and something can always complicate the situation. In aviation, there's a concept of a "point of no return": if a pilot passes this point, the aircraft won't have enough fuel to return to the same airfield. This term is also used in high-altitude mountaineering, where it means the point on a route after which, under certain, usually extreme, circumstances, the climber can no longer return down. And this happens because they no longer have the strength. It's the point where everything must be weighed and a decision made: to continue the ascent at the risk to health or life, or to concede defeat and descend. Fate once brought us to this point, but more on that later.

Usually, the challenge is simply to correctly assess and calculate your strength. The physical strain of ascending and descending is specific, affecting certain muscle groups and joints in ways they never experience under normal conditions. Did we think, starting our morning ascent to Bai Hua Mount's peak (6,532 feet), into what we would turn by evening descending the mountain? We became mere penguins, as our waddling gait most resembled these polar birds (here we coined the term "to penguinize"). We waddled because we couldn't bend our knees due to pain and walked on straight legs at a speed of no more than 1-2 mph - such was the effect of the steep ascent and then the lengthy descent. Our knees ached for another two weeks, then it seemed to pass. But as soon as we embarked on another trip, sharp pain returned after 60 miles, forcing us to change our goal from Mount Wutai to Mount Ling. Only after a couple of months of massage and Chinese ointment named Anmoru, recommended by our unforgettable Wushu teacher Liu Yunpeng, champion of China in Sanda, did our knee joints return to normal.

A mountaineer moves up the mountain unhurriedly, conserving energy at every movement, but continuously, making only planned brief stops at certain intervals. However, high-altitude climbers always go to the mountains for several days, while reaching mid-altitude peaks often takes just one day. Considering that we have already ascended several hundred feet above sea level on our way to the mountain, we can say that for peaks up to 7,000 feet in terrain (i.e., without any roads or paths) and descent, one day is enough. If the peak is up to 8,000 feet, one day suffices to visit and descend, provided there is some kind of road or trail. For heights of 8,000 - 10,000 feet, one day is often not enough. Unlike high-altitude climbers, we ascend at a faster pace, almost storming the mountain. But all our experience says that you should never rush or overestimate your strength during an ascent, that you should always be able to stop in time in a mountain village to continue the ascent the next day, no matter how close the goal seems.

Regarding food, during an ascent, one should carry only the bare minimum necessary, but what must be taken care of is a supply of water. The body's need for water increases with altitude.

In the very technique of moving across terrain, it's best to follow proven principles of mountaineering: check your support, three points of support, further from the rock - closer to the rock, etc. - we think it's unnecessary to explain these principles, familiar to everyone.

7/ Entering a city

What to say about entering a city after several days of trekking? Everything seems strange and hectic after the free mountains. You can't just stop on the side of the road, instead, you need to look for distinctive buildings with silhouettes of a man and a woman. And again, there will certainly be some racer on a shoddy bicycle, who's never traveled beyond the nearest store, trying patriotically to overtake the foreign devils. But I must say, with us, even returning from a thousand-miles tour, only a master of cycling could manage that.

8/ Stops for food and overnight

As we mentioned, both food and lodging can be easily found in most Chinese villages. The exceptions are remote, secluded places, off the roads and away from civilization, where to the local people, you truly appear as a devil. The most convenient for stopping for lunch or dinner are roadside villages, where someone is surely earning by feeding and watering drivers of passing vehicles, mainly lamèidì. You can easily recognize such an establishment by its sign. There, for a very cheap price, unimaginable in Beijing, you can snack or, if you wish, simply stuff yourself.

The names of dishes and their prices are often written on the wall or chalked on a blackboard. There's no accounting for taste: don't be surprised to see, for example, steamed sparrows, fried locusts, boiled squirrels, dog meat soup, etc., on such a board. The richness of Chinese cuisine is well-known. However, from this richness, you can always choose something edible.

Always ensure that the price of each dish is clearly marked and there is no space left for ambiguity or misinterpretation: in some diners, they will not hesitate to deceive and overcharge you, suddenly declaring at the end of your meal that that dish costs not five yuan per large plate, which you just ate, but five yuan per jin[15], and there were three jins in the plate. Also, order dishes precisely, without any vagueness that could be interpreted by the owners to their advantage. I remember arriving in Dengfeng county near Shaolin monastery, we ordered chicken - so they brought us an entire boiled chicken, placed with broth in a basin, the kind used for washing clothes. And they took money, of course, for the whole chicken, although we ate less than a quarter of it (it was, of course, finished later by other visitors).

It should be noted that blatant cheating often flourishes in various backwater towns, villages near cities, and areas popular with "moral freaks" on excursions. In such places, especially in the mountains, they are likely to try selling local "game" at triple the price. For example, they may offer a "leopard's leg," which turns out to be merely a fried cat, or a "pheasant," which is actually a dead chicken. But in more remote villages, where they haven't seen foreign devils, you won't encounter attempts to cheat.

Experience also shows that in financial matters, it's al- ways better to deal with a man, not a woman. I remember the following episode: once we ended up staying overnight in a village hospital, which we mentioned before. The caretakers were an old man and his wife. We were invited to join them for dinner, but since we had already dined earlier in another village, we just had tea. However, we sat with the hosts. And then, sitting on the kang and participating in the general conversation, we caught the wife quietly asking the old man how much to charge us for the night. "Just ten each, and that's all," he replied just as quietly. They were sure we hadn't heard or understood their brief dialogue. We should add that a price of ten yuan per night was quite fair. Imagine our surprise when in the morning the wife told us a completely different price: 50 yuan. And when we gave her a hundred note, she didn't come out with the change for about ten minutes, hoping, apparently, that we would get tired of waiting and leave - perhaps, in her mind, there was no particular difference between 50 yuan and a hundred for foreign devils. The old man, apparently out of shame, had disappeared altogether during this scene. Of course, we didn't say a word of reproach to the greedy old woman, but we also didn't bother to say "thank you" and "goodbye" - we just turned around and left. And this scene is not unique: whenever there's a need to fleece a traveler for more money, a woman takes the stage, while her husband prefers to disappear somewhere, either out of shame for his wife's greed and unable to restrain her, or showing that he has nothing to do with it.

Much depends, of course, on the village you end up in. In some places, the entire village gathers to look at us. Particularly memorable in this respect was Taipingbao, located beyond the Sea-Buckthorn Mountain: there, so many people popped out of every nook and cranny at the sight of us that it was hard to get through, the elderly were carried out into the street to have a look at the foreign devils once in their lifetime, and children followed us along the road for couple of miles (one of them tried to stick a stick in our wheel). Oh, these children from Chinese villages - you better not know what they sometimes shout after passing travelers. An overly warm welcome then leads to a crowd of onlookers and tedious inquiries (you can imagine how it feels to answer the same questions like "Where are you from?", "Where are you going?" etc., hundreds of times) - nothing could be worse after a hundred miles and mountain passes, when all you want is food and rest.

You can also get into a difficult situation when hospitable hosts, out of generous hearts, start treating you to their favorite delicacies. This happened to us in the county town of Yuxian, where we stopped at a wonderful, exemplary inn and were greeted warmly. This inn was also memorable for the only unisex public toilet we ever saw in China. What's that? - you might ask. At the toilet entrance, there's a board on a string, with "M" written on one side and "F" on the other - so, the nature of the toilet, so to speak, changes according to your wish - all you have to do is turn the board over. The owner, despite the late hour, invited us to dinner at his own inn, and kept treating us to various dishes. He was so polite and attentive to us that it was simply uncomfortable to refuse, even though we were already full. And at the end of dinner, the host joyfully announced: "And now - the main delicacy! I'll treat! Fried cow intestine with pepper!" You can imagine our state at this (the intestine also seemed poorly washed to us).

Once, we ended up in a village, remembered for the absolute equanimity of its inhabitants, which we nicknamed "The Village of Pythons." It happened one night on our return from Datong. We were looking for the village of Gu Ding Qiao to stay the night: on the map, the village was right on the road, but in reality, we only noticed it by a faint light visible nearly a mile away. Approaching the village, we couldn't find that light anymore - in fact, there was nothing resembling an inn or a lodging house. Moving along the edge of the village, we only saw a dimly yellow-lit window in the darkness once. But then a figure loomed ahead, and we asked it about lodging. The response was brief: "Follow me," and the figure led us to that very lighted window.

The door opened, and we found ourselves in a small house, where two old men, a knitting woman, and a young boy sat on stools, watching an old black-and-white TV. The TV reception was terrible, but the viewers were very patient. At our arrival, everyone turned for a couple of seconds and then, as if nothing had happened, stared back at the screen - you'd think foreigners on bicycles visit them every night. The next phrase we heard in this village was: "Sit down." After which, we were offered tea. As we sipped our tea, the hosts continued watching TV, not even turning around, though the boy did steal a couple of glances at us. Half an hour passed, and the question followed: "Will you eat?" Of course, we said yes. They brought us a modest dinner - modest in terms of the food, but not the quantity. When we finished, another and last question in this village was asked: "When will you go to sleep?"

For the night, we were allocated an empty, unfinished room. We again experienced the character of the village's residents when we were woken early in the morning in our room by some noises. Opening our eyes, we saw a lad with a tool in his hands standing in front of us. Noting our awakening, he simply said: "I work here." Following local customs, we, without asking anything (like why the heck he woke up the guests at the crack of dawn and couldn't wait an hour with his work), silently got up, dressed, and went outside. After an equally taciturn breakfast, they charged us a modest fee, after which our positive impression of the village was firmly established. One can only wish there were more such villages in China.

As for cities, a true rider on a trek rarely enters them, and they are usually backwater and out of the way. Staying overnight here should be in some hotel, but there's nothing interesting in them: sleepy maids, broken plumbing, curtains used as handkerchiefs. Perhaps the only hotel worth mentioning is the one where we had to spend a night in Datong, and that's only because of its name. It was called "Five Types of Love" (Wu Ai Binguan). What would you think, seeing such a name? We had the same thoughts. It turned out everything was completely different: Five Types of Love referred to love for the party, the people, the motherland, etc. – I don't remember what else.

DANGERS LURKING FOR A
RIDER ON THE ROAD

As in our everyday lives, they are numerous and unexpected. One of the most serious, perhaps, is getting lost at night in the darkness. As an example, I can cite our wanderings around Yuxian, which can also be classified as mysterious incidents.

That morning, we left the village of Gu Ding Qiao, reaching Guanglin by midday, and from there, we headed straight to Yuxian, a small county town near the border of Hebei and Shanxi provinces. We had already passed through Yuxian once, entering from a different direction. That time, what struck us most was a statue of some hero, towering at the town's eastern entrance, with the inscription "Wolf Tooth, Strong Man" on its pedestal. To the east of Yuxian lies a flat area, but now we were approaching from the west, descending from a mountain plateau.

On the map, just couple of miles west of the town, lies the village of Nuanquan ("Warm Spring"). Dusk was falling. Dark hamlets began to appear; the road forked in several directions. Spotting a figure moving ahead, we decided to ask for directions. The figure mumbled something incomprehensible and gestured insistently for us to follow to the right. We looked closer and realized it was just a local madman. However, a seemingly normal-looking auntie appeared out of nowhere and pointed us left.

After a couple of extremely winding turns, we entered Warm Spring village. This place left a lasting impression due to the spectacle we witnessed there. For some reason, the whole village was engulfed in evening twilight, probably due to some electrical issue. Suddenly, we found ourselves on the main street. Illuminated by candles and torches, accompanied by the lively music of a brass band, a large procession moved rapidly, carrying something like banners. The street itself, lively at such a late hour, shining with numerous candle-lights and kerosene lamps, did not resemble a typical street in a Chinese village at all. It was stone-paved, unusually wide, and in the darkness, even something like glass shopfronts glistened - it was utterly unbelievable. And most importantly, we did not understand the reason for all these festivities: there was no holiday that day, it looked neither like a wedding nor a funeral. In an instant, it felt as if we had been transported to another, almost mythical world.

We managed to cross the street just in front of the procession's head, paused for a moment to observe the strange scene. Unfortunately, we couldn't linger as we were eager to reach Yuxian before complete darkness fell, leaving the mystery of what we saw there unsolved.

As soon as we left the bizarre street, the village almost immediately ended. Darkness fell quickly. But we weren't worried, as Yuxian was just a stone's throw away. For a while, we rode on a gravel road illuminated in the darkness, lined with tall poplars rustling in the wind. Then, leading nowhere, the road gradually faded, and soon we completely lost it. Assuming we were no more than a mile from our destination, we decided to head straight east. But then, the terrain became increasingly complex, with water-filled ditches, dams, embankments, and sinkholes forcing us to circle in place. Eventually, we found ourselves in front of a structure looming in the darkness, which turned out to be an unfinished bridge. Without much thought, we picked up our bicycles and stepped onto the concrete skeleton of the bridge. Balancing on a concrete overlay no more than ten inches wide with our bicycles, like acrobats with poles, we crossed the bridge in about twenty steps. Although the stony bed of a dried river lay twenty feet below, we didn't think about the risk at that moment.

Crossing the bridge, we began to discern flickering lights in the darkness, and soon the illuminated Yuxian unfolded before us, no more than a mile away. Standing on an elevation, it was as if it lay in the palm of our hand; we could even make out the driver's inn where we had previously stayed. All that remained was to descend, find a suitable eatery, stretch our legs weary from the 100 miles day's journey, enjoy dinner, and relish a local beer. However, our trials were just beginning!

Over the next two to three hours, we experienced what it means to be totally mixed up: constantly seeing the lit town right under our noses, we futilely attempted to reach it. No matter where or how we went, an obstacle invariably emerged, forcing us to make detour after detour: a deep ditch, a narrow channel, a mound. We wandered in circles, unable to maintain our direction, and found ourselves repeatedly at the same spot. All this time, I repeat, the town was right before us, which started to seriously fray our nerves.

Finally, we made a determined attempt to break out of this bewitched circle. Veering sharply to the left, we entered a surreal landscape: black poles, as tall as a man or taller, protruded from the ground everywhere - it was a sorghum field. It was December, and the sorghum had been harvested, leaving behind its dried, stick-like, thick stems. Navigating through this field was extremely difficult - we had to clear our way by breaking through the barrier of stems, avoiding the sharp remnants jutting from the ground. Moreover, our noisy progression through the dry sorghum attracted the attention of the field's owners: suddenly, several large and ferocious dogs began barking furiously to our right, followed by a light turning on. A minute later, a hoarse voice, amplified by a megaphone and shouting something threatening in the local dialect difficult for us to understand, echoed across the field. The main message was clear: we were being ordered to leave the field immediately, or else the dogs would be unleashed and shots fired.

The peasants apparently decided to intimidate unknown persons wandering near their homes at night. They could have fulfilled at least the first part of their threat, if not the second. What to do – retreat from the field? But how much longer could we wander in circles?

Regardless of the threats and angry barking, we continued to push forward through the sorghum.

Soon, the field ended, and a semblance of a trail appeared, which we decided to follow without deviation, as it had to lead somewhere. Eventually, it brought us to a paved road. By then, the lights of the town had completely disappeared, and darkness surrounded us – it was about midnight. After cycling a few miles and circling north of Yuxian, we finally entered the town at midnight. So, as you can see, we faced the dangers of falling from a height of twenty feet onto rocks and an encounter with several vicious dogs (we only had one knife between the two of us).

Generally, the number of dangers and the likelihood of encountering them increases with the onset of darkness. For example, one night we were caught on a deserted road stretching across a vast plain with hardly any cars. It was silent. But then we heard a noise from behind, and soon a truck overtook us. In its bed was something large, angular, and protruding beyond its dimensions, so the sides of the bed were lowered. As soon as the truck had moved about 30 feet ahead of us, a sharp, deafening metallic crash echoed across the steppe, followed by the screech of brakes. We immediately braked too. Approaching the truck, we discovered that a huge metal plate, apparently part of some large machine, had fallen onto the road. The driver had already climbed out with a flashlight, and of course, as we passed by, we did not hesitate to curse him out. We could only thank God that the plate hadn't fallen earlier. And, of course, it goes without saying that had it been daytime, we would have immediately noticed the plate dangerously sliding towards the edge of the bed.

As for the mountains, nightfall promises an encounter with a leopard. These cunning beasts hunt for prey at night, silently approaching their victim within jumping distance be- fore attacking. You should know that when a leopard attacks a person, it jumps on his back or chest, sinking his teeth into his neck and striking with his hind legs. Climbing the Sea Buckthorn Mountain on a cold night in 19..., we suddenly heard faint movement in the bushes lining the road, and something black smoothly glided in the moonlight. Drawing our knife and talking loudly to each other, we passed the suspicious spot. The leopard did not dare attack us, probably because there were two of us.

In general, there are three main dangers in the mountains of China: leopards, dushé, and miners (not counting the possibility of falling from cliffs, slipping on glaciers or ice, and again falling down, rockfalls, etc.). We've already mentioned leopards, dushé are poisonous snakes, and miners require some explanation (Note: the following three paragraphs are not suitable for readers under 18 years of age).

Once, we had no idea of the danger posed by miners and what this danger entailed. Fortunately, back then, we hadn't been to the mountains, where many coal mines are located. It was a fine Siberian lad, Sasha from a village near town of Bodaibo, Russia, who first told us about this. There are many gold mines in Bodaibo area, and it was this fact that drove Sasha to choose mining as his profession. Inexplicably, his studies led him to China, to the Beijing Mining Institute. We often drank tea with Sasha, nibbling on the cakes baked by his wife Anya, listening to his tales of the taiga and gold mining.

Sasha disappeared for a whole month once: it was time for field practice, and he went to a coal mine. Upon his return, he shared the following story. While underground, he took a detour into a side shaft, where students were never taken, and to his surprise, in the light of his lantern, he saw used condoms scattered on the shaft floor. From that day, Sasha began to pay closer attention to the miners and their lifestyle. And what did he see? He started noticing things he hadn't before: particularly, how affectionately the miners treated each other. However, this affection was expressed with the miners' inherent roughness, sometimes they even indulged in rather playful jokes. For instance, once in a cramped elevator cage, one miner took out a condom, inflated it, and stuffed it under his friend's robe, simulating a woman's breast. When he began to "fondle" this "breast," his friend did not resist but showed feigned embarrassment. Their comrades found this entire scene hilariously entertaining. However, the miners restrained themselves around the interns and didn't allow anything similar.

Later, we learned about the abnormal disproportion in China's population between the number of men and women - the latter being significantly fewer and thus in shortage (we won't discuss the reasons for this disparity here), the low prestige of the miner's profession, and the challenging life in isolated male mining communities.

Once, a road in the foothills of Bai Hua Mountain led us through a mining camp. We had to pass through it. Fortunately, it was working hours, and almost no one was on the surface in the camp. Thus, we were only noticed when we had crossed the camp and were already climbing up. Miners resting in the barracks then poured out, staring at us intently. They looked extremely agitated and were discussing something. We exchanged glances and quickened our pace. But higher up, near the mine entrance, we encountered a miner in full underground gear. We passed him very closely, just couple feet away. However, he was alone and only followed us with a greedy gaze.

Since then, we've carefully avoided roads leading through mines. How can one recognize the dangerous proximity of miners? Blackened land from coal doesn't necessarily mean anything: it could just be a coal transshipment base. What should raise alarm are trolleys and pipes leading into the mountains - they supply water to the mines.

Remembering Bai Hua Mountain, let's talk about an- other dangerous encounter in these mountains - with the tufei of Shijiaying (as we mentioned above, tufei means "local bandits.") To preface, overall, modern China is quite safe for travelers, and its population is friendly and hospitable. However, as the old Chinese saying goes, "snakes and dragons live in a mix," and among normal people, there will always be some degenerates.

In the foothills of Bai Hua Mountains lies the extensive village of Shijiaying. We arrived there late in the evening, quite exhausted from the journey, and thus stopped at the first inn we found on its deserted outskirts. The inn and eatery were run by a beardy guy who looked Korean, along with two streetwise lads, who greeted us amicably, and a couple of clearly non-local girls who were definitely not there just to wash dishes. We immediately sensed that this place was "shady," as they say. Our suspicions were later confirmed.

The next morning, leaving our bikes and some unnecessary gear at the inn, we set off to climb Bai Hua summit. Returning from the summit late in the evening, around 11 pm, in our "penguin" state mentioned earlier, we realized that at our slow pace, we would reach the inn well past midnight - it was still several miles away through the dark, backwater outskirts of the village. Therefore, we decided to hitch a ride. For some reason, many khaki-colored vehicles passed by. Four or five had already passed, but none stopped. It seemed they were afraid to pick up hitchhikers so late - quite atypical for China and somewhat odd to us.

Suddenly, one jeep having passed about 30 yards ahead, braked, reversed, and approached us. A bald-headed person with an extremely unpleasant face emerged. We also noticed three or four people inside the vehicle. In response to our request for a lift, he countered with a question: Where to? Here we made a mistake in revealing our exact destination, especially since it was quite noticeable - the first inn at the entrance to the village. In hindsight, we realized we shouldn't have specified our destination so precisely. We didn't get an answer to our question. Instead, the Unpleasant face began to boldly ask us more questions: Who are you? What are you doing here? Why did you stop at that inn? etc. We disliked him even more.

As you might guess, he did not get any answers from us, and we changed our minds about asking them for a ride - but then he himself began to obsessively offer to take us to the inn. Without saying a word, we simply turned around and continued along the road. Then we heard a sharp shout behind us, as he tried to sound as authoritative as possible: "Come here now!" Of course, we continued to walk calmly forward without reacting. Meanwhile, we exchanged a few words, agreeing on how to act in case of escalation. The overwhelming number of opponents, the possible presence of cold weapons, and the desolation of the place left us no choice but to instantly act to incapacitate them completely, without worrying about the consequences (followed by seizing the car and heading to the nearest police station - but not in the village! - to report the incident first). As always, we had a knife ready in our waist bag. We immediately forgot about our "penguin" state as if it had never existed.

However, no further action followed. The jeep moved on, passed us, and disappeared into the darkness. Soon after, we flagged down a lamèidì which gave us a lift to our destination. As we expected, the jeep was already there, and the Unpleasant face with his cronies was circling around our bikes, parked outside the inn's doors. Of course, they were securely locked and chained together.

We calmly walked to the entrance, ignoring a couple of shouts, checked our bikes for any damage, and found none. At the entrance, the Unpleasant face tried to grab my sleeve, but I jerked it away sharply. Entering the hall, we began to wash our dirtied hands as if nothing happened and then sat down at a table. The Unpleasant face joined us, while his lackeys stood apart - their dull rural countenance was depressing, yet it was clear they would instantly obey any command from their leader. We stuck to our strategy - ignoring the Unpleasant face, we began ordering dinner from the hosts.

The hosts behaved neutrally, inquiring about our mountain trip, but we immediately sensed their support - we were guests at their inn, and the law of hospitality was in effect. It was evident they had a talk with the Unpleasant face before our arrival.

The Unpleasant face intruded into our conversation again, bombarding us with questions: Where are you from? Do you have passports? The last question was very telling - both Victor and I had our experiences in this regard. Encountering a foreigner, Chinese hooligans and thugs often try to seize their documents. Once, a guy claiming to be a policeman on a dark street of Beijing demanded to see my ID. Sensing trouble for himself, he retreated in silence. Victor had a tougher experience in Canton when he naively let a thug see his Chinese residence permit. The thug demanded a ransom for its return. After a heartfelt conversation, the thug not only returned the document but also offered to join him in mugging someone.

You might wonder why Chinese thugs would want foreign IDs. Losing a passport abroad is not a huge inconvenience - you just report it to your embassy and get a new one or a temporary replacement. This question would only amuse someone in the know. A foreign passport can always be sold to people who lovingly alter it for their client's needs.

However, the Unpleasant face with his friends likely weren't involved in passport trading. They were just desperately looking for some leverage to blackmail us, to get something from us. But soon the Unpleasant face realized it was tough to get a hold of us, and the situation was not in his favor. Eventually, he and his dull cronies left the yard. The engine started, and the jeep sped back to Shijiaying.

By then, our table was laden with dumplings and snacks. One of the hosts came over and apologized for the Unpleasant face's behavior. We were fortunate to have stopped at this particular "shady" inn; elsewhere, where the owners feared the bandits, things might have turned out differently. Needless to say, we were grateful to the hosts, especially since our steel steeds were intact. It turned out the Unpleasant face had tried to remove the number plate from one of the bikes (in China, akin cars, bikes are registered and have numbers, although not everyone there follows this law). The next morning, we left Shijiaying.

Once, a road led us to another tufei village in Shanxi province, where grim warnings for travelers were written on trees, and gratitude was expressed to a certain "grandfather" (akin to a local godfather) for protecting the village. We stopped there for dinner, but no incidents occurred.

So, it is indeed at night, with the onset of darkness, that the likelihood of encountering some danger, whether natural or human, increases. And indeed, we found ourselves in the most perilous situation during our travels at night. But more on that later.

MYSTERIOUS ENCOUNTERS ON OUR JOURNEYS

Under mysterious encounters, we refer to those that defied rational explanation, making us contemplate the existence of otherworldly or higher powers that occasionally make their presence felt in our lives. Here, we'll narrate a couple of such instances; the first will appeal to those enamored with Eastern exoticism, steeped in the religions and martial arts of the East, while the second, we hope, will prove to be quite instructive.

So, the first case. In the summer of 19..., we embarked on an ascent to the summit of Ling Mountain (7,555 feet), located 125 miles west of Beijing. Ling means "Spirit, Soul" and it's the highest point in the Beijing municipality. The mountain is famous for its extensive green alpine meadows at an elevation of 6,500 feet. A stony road leads up from the foothills, not quite reaching the summit. Back then, the road was being widened, with some blasting work in progress. It was this road we ascended, pushing our steel steeds.

Progress was challenging due to the extreme rockiness of the road, its steep gradient, and the lengthy distance exacerbated by constant switchbacks. We had been walking for over half a day, yet the summit remained hidden behind steep cliffs.

After another turn, we encountered a booth with a barrier. This was familiar to us: peasants sometimes set these up at the entrance to their lands, especially if the place has some minor fame, in hopes of collecting a fee from passing tourists. However, the barrier was raised, no movement was seen in the booth, so we continued unimpeded.

Just beyond the barrier was a straight, 200-yards stretch of road ascending sharply. Having climbed it and turned left, we noticed, about 100 yards behind us, a person had appeared. Where did he come from?

We had been alone all this time, not yet passing through any hamlets. "Must have come out of the booth," we thought.

At the next turn, the gap between us and the person had halved. Now we could see him clearly: an old man with a long grey beard, clad in simple peasant clothing. What you need to know, reader, is that although we had been walking up the mountain, pushing our steel steeds, for many hours, we nevertheless moved very quickly, since we were trying to get to the summit and go down before dark. "What a spry old man," we thought at the time.

Then, a steep switchback began. The road wound upwards in tight spirals along nearly vertical cliffs, each twist elevating it as high as a four-story building, with sheer rock slides in between. After negotiating the last twist, we stopped for a break. I approached the edge of the rock slide; the entire road lay below like in the palm of my hand. But then, I couldn't see the old man. "Where did the old man go?" I thought, turning to tell Victor about my observation. At that moment, I saw the old man. Now he was already 50 yards ahead of us on the road, and quickly moving away. Even from the back, his distinctive figure and gray head were unmistakable (and there was no one else around).

We were dumbfounded. Clearly, the old man hadn't overtaken us; besides the switchback, there were no other paths or trails; the only way to get ahead of us was to climb directly up the rock slides - but that would only be feasible for an experienced mountaineer or rock climber, and even then, they couldn't have outpaced us. And even if we assume there was a secret path known only to locals (though the area was clearly visible to us), the steepness would have made the ascent very challenging and time-consuming. We immediately hurried after the old man, who had disappeared behind a rock. Beyond the rock lay a hamlet, and the old man, moving with an unusually light and smooth gait (only now did we notice this!), entered the hamlet and vanished between the houses. It wasn't appropriate to follow him and ask for explanations. So, we continued upwards.

How to explain what we saw? Of course, Chinese Taoists came to mind: some of them, according to legends, could walk on sand without leaving traces, fly on clouds, etc. For a more realistic explanation, one could recall the Tibetan Lung Gom Pa runners, who had a special technique for swift movement in the mountains. However, the art of Lung Gom Pa has long been forgotten. And importantly, even if the old man used some special technique, apart from the switchback, he had no other way to ascend but through the rock slides, and any movement on them, regardless of the method, would have caused the sound of falling pebbles. But we heard no such sounds, only complete silence. To this day, this case remains an insoluble mystery for us.

The second case occurred in the summer of 19... While examining a map of Northern China's attractions, we stum- bled upon a Buddhist monastery on Mount Pan (just 2,835 feet), 75 miles east of Beijing, named Shaolin. Those even slightly familiar with Chinese Buddhism and Oriental martial arts need no introduction to the Shaolin Monastery in Henan province. As the monastery gained nationwide fame, it spawned namesakes: thus, distinguishing between Northern and Southern Shaolin appeared, and eventually, the number of monasteries bearing this name reached ten. Each served as a branch of the original monastery, preserving its "profile." The very name Shaolin obliges monks to practice martial arts, to live up to the legacy of their predecessors - once, Shaolin monks were considered unbeatable in hand-to-hand combat in China. Whether they still uphold this standard is another matter.

During our first year in China, we visited the original Shaolin in the Song Mountains of Henan Province. But we had no idea that another branch of the famous monastery was located so close to Beijing. There it was on the map, marked with pictogram of monastery gates, a pagoda, and three large characters - Shaolin Monastery, at the very center of Mount Pan. We immediately began planning our route.

It was very simple: an eastward road from Beijing leads straight there. Traveling 75 miles on it brings you to the county town of Jixian. Mount Pan lies about 12 miles before Jixian, to the left of the road. We were supposed to reach the village of Xipanzhuang via the road, turn left, and after traveling 12 miles, find ourselves at the gates of the monastery.

We knew we could cover this distance in a day, then we'd need to find a place to spend the night, and the next morning, head to Shaolin. Where to stay? We could reach Jixian (the map showed a pictogram of Buddhist temple with the inscription Duluo Monastery there), but what use was that town to us? Our goal was Shaolin, not Duluo. So, we decided, as usual, to find overnight lodging in one of the hamlets near Mount Pan.

East of Beijing, there are no high mountains; the road is flat and rather monotonous. This was our first journey to these parts, solely to visit Shaolin. Riding there was dull for true riders like us, used to steep ascents and descents and expansive mountain landscapes west of Beijing. Perhaps out of boredom, we felt inclined to jest. Duluo Monastery came to mind. Duluo translates as "Solitary Joy." What kind of joys did monks find alone there? - we asked ourselves and readily supplied quite indecent answer. So, we rode, cracking the most indecent jokes about Duluo all the way.

Meanwhile, evening fell, and in the darkness, we turned left at Xipanzhuang village, approaching Mount Pan, passing hamlets one after another and checking each against the map. About an hour later, we reached the last hamlet on this road, Yushizhuang, beyond which, just a mile away, lay the mountain itself. The hamlet seemed dark and out of the way, so we decided to keep going to the mountain, where we figured an inn would be, especially as it was just around nine in the evening.

We had a minor setback: in the darkness, we couldn't find the exit from the hamlet leading to Mount Pan. The village was completely engulfed in darkness, and there was no one to ask. Finally, we found an open shop; the owner explained that the exit to the paved road, leading to Mount Pan, was just a couple of steps away.

Having turned onto the paved road, we somehow quite naturally headed right. The asphalt made for easier riding, and we picked up speed. A hamlet passed by, then another. Then came a stretch of uninhabited land. But the mountain was nowhere in sight. However, we saw some distant lights on the left and expected the road to turn towards them, leading us straight to the mountain, but that moment never came. We began to realize we were headed in the wrong direction. Eventually, ten miles along this road, we found a signpost. It turned out we were heading towards Jixian, already close to it! No, Jixian was not our destination. After all, we hadn't come for Duluo.

Annoyed with ourselves, we turned around and retraced the ten miles back to Yushizhuang. After some thought, we realized we had taken the wrong turn on the paved road, although the left turn to Mount Pan had been blatantly obvious. We couldn't understand what made us turn right. But now we knew the correct way and soon stood at the Mount Pan signpost. However, despite scouting the area and searching for lights in the night, we couldn't find anywhere to stay. The nearby hamlet seemed to be asleep (it was around mid- night) – not a single light was visible. Moreover, all the houses were surrounded by stone walls, and the gates were locked: knocking would have been futile.

However, as we scouted the area, turning onto a dirt road near the hamlet, and cursing as we navigated through bumps in the absolute darkness, a rectangle of light suddenly flashed from an opening door. A silhouette appeared, barking at us: "What do you want here?" followed by: "Are you seeking death?" Under different circumstances, the silhouette, so clearly visible in the light of the door, might have received a response from us that would not have been pleasing. However, we had no time for that – with midnight approaching, we were still in search of a place to stay for the night. We didn't like these places and, as strange as it was to admit, our only option was to head to Jixian – the only place we were guaranteed to find accommodation.

For the third time, we took the same paved road, realizing that to reach Shaolin tomorrow, we'd have to traverse it a fourth time. About an hour later, Jixian began. We came upon a fork: one road seemed to lead to the town center, with residential buildings ahead, and another into the town but to an unclear destination. However, the second road had a sign: "Hotel" (I don't remember the exact name). We felt the shabby outskirts hotel was likely locked at such a late hour, and there was no chance of waking the sleeping watchman. It seemed safer to head to the town center. And we were about to do just that, but *something* (what?) made us choose the second path.

As you've guessed, the hotel was locked with a padlock. Moreover, the gates in its surrounding iron fence were also chained shut. We had no choice but to continue.

Soon after, the asphalt turned into cobblestone, and ahead, contrasting with the modest buildings of the county town, a tall arch in traditional Chinese style appeared. The cobblestone road led us right under this arch. To our astonishment, we seemed to have been transported back a couple of hundred years: right beyond the arch was a narrow, lantern-lit street, lined with ancient houses in traditional Chinese architectural style. A few dozen yards down the street, we came upon some gates, next to which was a stone plaque. And there, we stopped and read the inscription on the plaque. What was written? "Duluo Monastery." It was exactly one o'clock a.m.

Of course, within few minutes, we found a hotel and spent the night two blocks away from Duluo. Don't think that was the end of it. No, we still had to drain this cup to the dregs. The next morning, we found Jixian, deserted at night, bustling and full of people. After a quick bite, we headed towards the town exit. As you can imagine, our path again passed near Duluo. And we thought: since the road strangely led us directly to the monastery's gates last night, perhaps we should visit it. We hesitated upon learning that the visit cost 25 yuan – an exorbitantly high price for such a backwater as Jixian – but we paid anyway.

With a sense of anticipation, we entered those very gates - now we would discover what Duluo really was. And we learned. The monastery consisted of a single structure. But its appearance remained a mystery, as it was entirely enveloped in scaffolding and plastic sheets - under restoration. Of course, the swindlers at the ticket booth had not informed us of this. Besides the mentioned building, there was absolutely nothing else on the small monastery grounds: just a couple of shacks selling trinkets, and a public toilet. That was Duluo.

We could have demanded our money back and caused a commotion at the ticket booth, but at that moment, we had no inclination to do so. We simply sat on a small stone bench there, pulled out a can of peach compote from our backpack, and ate it. Twenty minutes later, we left Duluo mounted our steel steeds, and for the fourth time, headed on the now- familiar road to Mount Pan (thus, in total, we had fruitlessly traveled forty miles back and forth). A fantasy then entered our minds: in this area, the spirits of the Shaolin and Duluo monasteries have long been in conflict. It's hard to imagine two more suitable antipodes: the stern, ascetic, and martial Shaolin, and the solitary joy-seeking Duluo. Moreover, at moments, it seemed we could almost physically sense this confrontation on the foothills. But again, this was just fantasy, the sensations too vague and fleeting.

Soon, however, we arrived at Mount Pan, and our thoughts fully turned to Shaolin: we discussed whether we would have a chance to spar with the monks. Since we had a map of the mountain, and Shaolin was marked on it, finding the way posed no trouble. And so, we reached the spot: the mountains were covered in green crowns of trees, with a picturesque white pagoda rising above them. But, alas, no matter how hard we searched, we couldn't find Shaolin, even though, according to the map, we were undoubtedly near it. Could the white pagoda be related to it? We decided to climb towards it. On our way up, we met a local who, in response to our question about Shaolin, mumbled something unintelligible but pointed upwards, towards the pagoda. Encouraged, we climbed more eagerly. What a disappointment it was to find, at the top, nothing but a desecrated pagoda defaced with obscene words. No monastery gates, no main temple, no meditation hall, no training grounds for monks. Just an area covered in grass and shrubs, with odd earth mounds scattered about.

Everything became clear when we descended and met another local, this time a quite perceptive-looking young man. He told us that Shaolin had indeed been there but was completely destroyed during the war with the Japanese, and now only the white pagoda remained.

Two feelings dominated us then: a desire to kick ass of the person who compiled the map of North China's attractions, and more so - not a feeling, but a realization that the spirit of Duluo had achieved a complete victory over the spirit of Shaolin here. And the defiled white pagoda stood as a silent symbol of this victory on Mount Pan. Who knows, perhaps the spirit of Duluo had triumphed throughout China? Anyone familiar with modern China would understand that this question is not without merit.

We won't recount how we climbed to the summit of Mount Pan, only to find a vile gathering of "moral freaks," or how we returned to Beijing the same night. We'll also omit possible explanations for what happened to us. If the reader believes this was all a series of coincidences, they can be content with that explanation.

THE WUTAI LESSON

I decided to share with the reader our harsh journey to Wutai Mountain, as it demonstrates how seemingly in- significant miscalculations and inattention to details in mountain biking can lead to unpredictable and dangerous consequences. This expedition was a significant lesson for us, as we approached the dangerous line we previously discussed in the mountaineering section.

We had long dreamed of journey to Wutai, one of China's Four Sacred Buddhist Mountains, and the most sacred among them. Even today, there are about sixty active temples and monasteries in the area, the oldest dating back to the Song time (about 1,000 years ago). They survived the Cultural Revolution thanks to the relative inaccessibility of these mountains. Wutai is also famed for its martial arts traditions.

Wutai, meaning "Five Terraces," derives its name from five peaks towering like gigantic platforms in the center of this mountain range. The highest peak Edou (known also as Beitaiding) at 1,902 feet, is also the highest in Northern China. The entire range spans 155 square miles, located 250 miles southwest of Beijing in Shanxi Province. The "Five Terraces" form a ring, and between them located Taihuai, the only significant settlement in these mountains. That was our goal, as it's surrounded by the most renowned temples. After visiting the temples, we planned to ascend Edou peak.

We set off on February 6, exceptionally well-dressed for the cold, knowing that Wutai is also called the Cool Mountain. In January 1958, it registered the lowest temperature in Shanxi Province at -49F. According to our atlas of China, it even snows here in summer.

February 6 was significant, marking the Spring Festival - the Chinese New Year, the most important holiday for the Chinese. Celebrating this traditional festival in some unfamiliar village was expected to add a special touch to our journey.

We planned to first travel 250 miles over three days along State Road No.108 to the beginning of the Wutai Mountain Range, and then turn into the mountains to ascend towards Taihuai town. The route from the Road No.108 to Taihuai posed a question. To the north of Wutai Mountain lies Shahé, a railway station connected to Taihuai by a paved road. We could use it, as it's the only road to Taihuai marked on the maps. However, coming from Beijing, this route meant a 45-mile detour from the north. Examining the maps closely, we noticed a dirt road from the village of Shentangbao, on the Road No.108, heading towards Taihuai, ending a few miles later at Zhuangwang village.

We reasoned that the road marked for drivers ended at Zhuangwang because it was impassable for cars beyond that. But surely, village's centuries-old inhabitants must have found and trodden a path to Taihuai town. Where they could go, so could we, the riders of steel steeds. Thus, we chose the route through Zhuangwang.

Now, a mention of technical preparations is essential. The day before, I noticed that my bike's left Japanese pedal was not spinning freely. Dismantling it, I found that a couple of bearing balls had worn out, probably due to sand intrusion. There was no time to source new balls, so I replaced the pedals. I had two spare pairs, but one, seemingly too small for my foot, made me choose the other.

Their unfamiliar appearance and lack of a manufacturer's name or "Made in Japan/Taiwan" mark (as we noted, Japanese and Taiwanese bicycle parts dominate China's imports) were concerning. However, they were functional and had some Latin lettering and numbers, suggesting non - Chinese origin (my biggest fear). Despite some initial resistance when screwing them into the cranks, they fit, and I forgot my doubts.

We won't detail our three-day journey along Road No.108. We celebrated the Spring Festival in Jiaodaokou Village, marveling at unseen village sights like ancestor altars listing up to fifteen generations.

We enjoyed the quiet roads, devoid of cars due to the holiday, but struggled with closed eateries along the way. Our path through poor areas of Shanxi meant modest local diets and overpriced food and lodging. We also encountered the longest and most exhausting ascent of all our tours, stretching 30 miles (and done at night).

On the fourth morning, after a bite in a roadside shack in Shentangbao (or Santa Bu, as locals call it), we turned onto the dirt road into Wutai Mountain. That's when it happened: my bike's right pedal first lost its axis (costing us about an hour of precious time in attempted repairs) and then completely fell off due to a broken core. Upon inspection, there was no doubt about the pedals' origin: we knew where such steel - if it could even be called that - was cast, a mere alloy of various junk. You can imagine the harsh words echoing off the surrounding cliffs at that moment.

The question "What should we do" did not arise. The only hope to find a spare pedal (any!) lay in Taihuai, so we had to keep moving forward on foot to reach our destination. It should be mentioned that by that time, we were deeply immersed in the mountains, in a rather wide (about 100 yards) gorge, surrounded by tall, sheer cliffs. At the gorge's base flowed a frozen mountain river, beside which we walked, slowly ascending to greater heights.

Initially a dirt road, it became increasingly rocky, eventually turning into a mere stone path. We passed a certain hamlet. All dwellings here were surrounded by high walls made of cobblestones, abundant in the gorge, with double gates tightly closed even during the day. Agriculture in this stony sack was done by clearing large stones from a plot, enclosing it with stones again, and bringing in soil from somewhere, possibly the mountains, to fill the formed bed, creating a furrow. Besides, sheep were kept here. No people were visible, though. Finally, we noticed a peasant – he was rinsing clothes in the thawed part of the river – and asked him how far it was to Taihuai. "Forty li," he replied (twelve miles).

After passing the hamlet, the stones in the gorge grew larger, and the path became more and more indistinct and difficult to navigate. Moreover, it led upwards more steeply. We had to choose carefully where to step and where to roll the bicycle. About two hours later, we found ourselves at a crossroads: the gorge and the road forked. Of course, there were no signs, and not a soul around. We had long passed the point where this road was marked on the map and had to rely solely on our intuition. After some thought, we turned left.

By evening, as the day began to wane, we arrived at another small and extremely remote hamlet – the power line that had accompanied us through the gorge ended here. Even if my bike had been working, we couldn't have ridden our steel horses steeds here due to the extreme rockiness and steep ascent – we could only walk. The three villagers we encountered, dressed in blue-green pants and jackets reminiscent of Mao's era, were not particularly welcoming: they repeatedly ignored our persistent question about whether we were heading correctly to Taihuai and how much farther it was. The only response was, "Tsou bu dao" (You won't make it). Eventually, one of them grudgingly answered. We were quite surprised, as he said: "Forty li" (twelve miles). Thus, according to these words, we had walked half a day but had not gotten any closer to Taihuai.

On the outskirts of the hamlet, we came across another local, a much friendlier old man, who clearly confirmed that we were going in the right direction. However, he warned us that the road ahead was difficult and that we would have to carry our bicycles. He also advised us to rest at a place ahead, which we didn't quite understand due to the local dialect. But the knowledge that something lay ahead gave us some confidence – it was more cheerful to walk, as after this hamlet, we were surrounded by completely wild terrain, the frozen river disappeared, and the gorge became even steeper.

Exiting the hamlet, we were amused by the local don- keys. A trio of them scampered away in panic, heading up the gorge away from us. Although there was enough space to bypass us, they stubbornly climbed upwards. They would run about 50 yards, stop and wait – as if we might stop and turn back – and upon our approach, they would rush up the stones again. "Well," we thought, "since the inhabitants of this hamlet were so inhospitable to us, let's drive their donkeys into the mountains!" However, after a mile, the donkeys found a safe spot, according to them, and passed us on the left, keeping as far away as possible.

Again, the ascent along the stony bottom of the gorge stretched out. We entered it in the morning, and now the sun threatened to soon disappear behind the ridge we constantly saw ahead. We carefully watched this ridge, searching for signs of an approaching pass. Looking back, we saw the mountains lying far below, lit by the setting sun – sheer mountains – as we had ascended quite high during the day, by our estimates, above 6,500 feet, and considering the height of the Wutai Mountains, the pass had to be near.

Suddenly, about two hours later, we again noticed a hamlet ahead, consisting of about ten houses. We had not yet encountered such a remote place – the hamlet wasn't even electrified and thus darkly loomed among the rocks in the evening. It could only be reached on foot by the same road that had brought us there (or by helicopter, descending into the hamlet by rope ladder, as there was nowhere for a helicopter to land). The gorge here narrowed significantly – it was clear that we were approaching its beginning. This was apparently where the old man below had advised us to rest.

However, we didn't stop at the hamlet for two main reasons: first, its appearance did not seem welcoming for an overnight stay, and second, more importantly, ahead in the mountain ridge at the gorge's entrance, we saw a ridge rise, beyond which there appeared to be no higher point (except for a distant snow-capped peak, which we surmised to be one of the "Five Terraces" – the Eastern Peak). This meant that the pass, opening the descent to Taihuai, was on the ridge, which was very close, just within reach. Although the sun had already set behind it, it was still light enough to make the final push and climb up.

Let me tell you, we had been moving through the gorge all day without so much as a poppy seed in our mouths – of course, there were no eateries here, and our desire to quickly reach Taihuai, where we could drink and eat, also drove us forward. After the trials of the past four days, we even dreamed of a hotel. So, increasing our pace even more, we pressed on upwards. However, we couldn't exactly rush – let's say we tried to rush – fatigue was taking its toll (after all, a day of climbing to a height of 6,500 or more feet over stones, pushing and sometimes carrying bicycles, without water or food, was no joke).

Now our path lay along a narrow trail, in places not wide enough to roll the bicycle alongside. Soon our situation began to worsen: it quickly darkened, the path went very steeply uphill, and to top it all off, it began to snow. But it was the snow, falling like a white retouch on the ground and stones, that helped us make out the path when it got completely dark. Despite everything, we stubbornly continued to climb upward. The view of the mountains ahead, discernible in the darkness again thanks to the snow, changed: the ridge sharply approached, grew in size, but moved to the left, the gorge, having finally narrowed to a black slit, remained below – now we were climbing along a steep (about 60 degrees) slope. Now we were almost level in height with the whitening ridge on the left, from which we were now separated by the gorge, transformed into a chasm. Thanks to this, as well as the steepness of the slope, we felt that we were at a considerable height – possibly above 8,200 feet. And then the first critical moment arrived: we lost the trail.

Frankly, it was hard to tell when we lost the path – per- haps it happened much earlier. We realized we had mistaken the white stripes of snow, bordering rows of thorny bushes on the slope, for a trail. For a while, we tried to find the path, but quickly understood it was futile. In the darkness, we couldn't even discern where we came from or find our way back. Looking around, we noticed the slope we were on seemed to end about 50-100 yards up – there, the boundary between the black mountain and the not-quite-black sky was discernible. So, we decided to climb up directly, hoping to survey our surroundings from above and determine our location. This ascent demanded tremendous effort: we had to literally hack our way through dense thickets of dry, intertwined thorny bushes; one of us went ahead clearing the path, then took the bicycles from the other in turns – advancing only 3-6 feet in 5-10 minutes. Most importantly, our strength was waning, the bicycles felt unbelievably heavy, and our hands trembled while lifting them. That's when I truly grasped, tangibly, that a person's reserve of strength and endurance has its limits. I understood how climbers perish in the mountains because they have no strength left for the descent. Our endurance was not yet at its limit, but we keenly felt that if we continued such an ascent, it would quickly diminish. The desire to simply sit down and remain seated emerged. And even if we had managed to reach the top of the slope, we didn't know what awaited us above.

We halted our climb and sat down on the rocks. Snow was falling. Perhaps never before had I felt such detachment from civilization and lostness in the mountains as I did then. This was the second critical moment. Gradually we realized: to move further, we first had to part with our bicycles. We couldn't carry them uphill – we lacked the strength; nor could we descend with them – risking stumbling and falling into an abyss. Needless to say, we had never experienced this neither before nor after.

Similar to sailors opening the Kingston valve, we untied the backpack from the luggage rack and abandoned our steel steeds on the mountain slope. There they lie, Wild Cat and Diamond Ass, perhaps to this day in the Wutai Mountains, unless someone from that non-electrified hamlet found them. However, for such a lucky guy, they would be as useful as glasses to a monkey, since even mountain biking is impossible in those places.

As bitter as it was to part with our steel steeds, we understood that by doing so, we were possibly saving our lives. Now, unburdened, we continued upward. This was the third critical moment, as continuing to move upward was a dangerous mistake. However, we eventually realized this – after all, we were moving completely without bearings, into nowhere, simply hoping to eventually reach a pass – but our desire to reach Taihuai at all costs was too strong. However, this way, we risked spending the entire night high in the mountains, constantly moving to avoid freezing, and ending up somewhere unknown – fortunately, not at the bottom of an abyss (we had already nearly slipped on the wet, snowy stones a couple of times, as a person's coordination deteriorates with fatigue). Thus, the only viable option was evacuation. More precisely, self-evacuation, as calling a helicopter by radio, as you understand, was not an option for us.

Unlike the ascent, during the descent, we had to end up somewhere specific – in the gorge we had climbed, as there were no other paths here. Now our way lay only downwards. And here, snow helped us again. Firstly, we were terribly thirsty – and the snow quenched our thirst. I dare not say how much snow we ate then, and no one caught a cold afterward. Secondly, the slope we entered was so steep and slippery that it was most convenient to descend on the buttocks – of course, choosing a suitable route for this and constantly securing ourselves with hands and feet.

The snow seemed to pave smooth paths for us to slide down and generally retouched the slope, marking stones, bushes, cliffs, and crevices. Thus, devouring handfuls of snow, we slid down, straining our eyes in the dark to avoid accidentally slipping into an abyss. This descent lasted a long time; we kept marveling at how high we had climbed! One slope ended, we crossed a crevice onto the second and slid down again, then moved to the third. A couple of times, black voids of steep cliffs appeared ahead, then we had to brake and look for detours. We didn't recognize the place we ended up in. Finally, under our feet (or rather, our buttocks), something like a path appeared. It led us down for a long time, now at a less steep angle, and eventually, we were able to walk.

Soon enough, we literally stumbled upon agricultural terraces: I stepped over a stone ridge, only to find no support behind it, leading to my falling down. The fall, however, was short – only five feet. Here, the snow, on the contrary, concealed the terraces, and we fell 2-3 more times until we got used to the new terrain's relief. We walked through the terraces for a long time, endless terraces stretching downward. A jump down, ten steps forward, another jump down, ten steps forward – and so on, many, very many times – until the terraces became smaller and eventually disappeared, and behind them, as expected, we stumbled upon a fanza in the dark. It may seem strange to you, but at that moment we were in the best and most uplifted mood – despite it being 2 a.m., and we hadn't eaten for almost a day, in the middle of nowhere in the mountains – because we had avoided mortal danger and finally descended!

We didn't stand on ceremony and began knocking on the gates, doors, and windows of all the houses in the hamlet that we could approach (most houses were surrounded by a stone wall, and the gates were securely locked). But there was no response to our knocking and voices, not a single sound. Whether we were taken for bandits or devils, not a single soul in that hamlet dared to open a door, let alone respond. Well, we decided to go down until we came out of the mountains, no matter when. To our joy, moving forward, we recognized by certain signs that we were in the same non-electrified hamlet.

Now, evacuation was just a matter of patience and legs. Both were severely tested that night. The stones constantly under our feet in the dark were particularly annoying – it was easy to twist an ankle on them. That night, we simply hated the stones. We found our way among the stones almost intuitively. By morning, when it got light, we moved in silence, not talking to each other, like two sleepwalkers. I walked ahead, Victor – about thirty steps behind. All our thoughts were focused on walking, food, and water. However, there was no clarity in thoughts; I seemed to fall asleep while walking and even saw several dreams. Victor told me I was staggering (but how was he walking himself?). We perked up when we saw a bridge ahead – it was the exit to the Road No.108. Thus, by 8 a.m., we arrived in Santa Bu. Later, we calculated that in 24 hours of continuous movement, without water and food, we covered at least 60 miles having climbed to an altitude of about 8,200 feet, and then descended.

What followed – our time drinking peach compote in Santa Bu, hiring a car for 300 yuan to the Shahe station, boarding a train in Shahe, and arriving in Beijing by evening – doesn't merit a detailed recounting. It's worth noting, how- ever, that we found Shahe unappealing, a dismal, windswept place on the steppe with only one open eatery, a grimy corner serving nothing but poor-quality instant noodles and a few eggs. Upon arriving in Beijing, we headed straight to American restaurant named Frank's place and indulged in a substantial feast of various foods.

This brings us to the end of our challenging journey to the Wutai Mountains. We acknowledge that we left out certain aspects, especially our thoughts on mountains and mountain biking during the nocturnal evacuation, while conversation was still possible.

ON THE PERILS OF DECEPTION

Of course, having left our bikes on Mount Wutai and returned to Beijing, we couldn't just rest. We immediately set about acquiring parts and assembling new bicycles to venture back to Mount Wutai, this time determined to reach it. As it would be boring to take the same route again, we decided to change our path and do something we had never done before. On a cold February morning, we boarded a train at Beijing's South Station, bound for Shahe, with our steel steeds disassembled and packed in large bags, which we placed on the train floor. At Shahe Station, we planned to quickly assemble our bicycles and head out on the only paved road leading directly to the town of Taihuai, the heart of the Mount Wutai region, overcoming a pass at 8200 feet. By our calculations, we should have reached Taihuai by nightfall.

The train journey, slow and punctuated with frequent stops, was monotonous, memorable only for a group of eight guys playing cards throughout, who, when checked, turned out to be without tickets and refused to buy them. Neither the two conductors nor the summoned police officer could do anything with them. Apparently, they were tufei, returning from Beijing to their native village.

By evening, we finally arrived at Shahe. I've already mentioned this windy, ice-cold place in the steppes, where the only food available was poor-quality instant noodles and eggs.

However, we had already eaten on the train. You should know that in all Chinese trains, various foods are constantly carted around, and while not the pinnacle of Chinese cuisine, they're hot and filling. After assembling our bikes at the station, we set off immediately.

The landscape was completely snow-free. The road headed straight north, and after about two hours, we reached the start of an ascent that soon made cycling impossible. Dis- mounting, we pushed our steel steeds uphill on foot.

Around midnight, a snowstorm began. In the total darkness, the empty road, where we saw neither tractors nor cars, snaked up in long serpentines, but we couldn't seem to reach the pass. It became clear we wouldn't reach Taihuai until around 3 a.m. So, when a dim light followed by the headlights of a car appeared behind us, we immediately decided to try flagging the car down – this being only the second time we had done so on all our trips.

It was a black Soviet "Volga" (at that time, Soviet cars were common in China). The driver and the sole passenger quickly agreed to take us to Taihuai. Luckily, the "Volga" had a very large trunk, which was empty, so our steel steeds fit inside, albeit with the front wheels removed. A few minutes later, we were sitting in the back seat, recovering from the exhausting night climb through the snowstorm.

As we drove, we chatted with the "Volga" passenger – a man about 45 who made a good impression on us. Naturally, we answered his numerous questions about what on earth we were doing on a mountain road in a snowstorm, miles from the nearest habitation, and soon the conversation turned to who we were and what we were doing in China. I must tell you, reader, that at that time both Victor and I lived in Beijing with residence permits. In China at that time, this was a document like a passport, only smaller and green, stating the address and occupation of the foreigner. Since we were working as managers in trading companies at the time, one could easily find out by opening our green booklets, which, in case of a check by the authorities, we carried with us.

So, when the friendly "Volga" passenger asked what we were doing in Beijing, Victor and I exchanged glances and told him we were poor students studying Mandarin. Why did we want to hide our true status? The question was about money. So far, the driver hadn't said a word about payment for the ride, but we knew the issue might arise when we arrived. So, to be asked for less, we claimed to be students. As you can imagine, the fare expected from managers of a foreign trading company, who are commonly perceived in China as making substantial money, would be significantly different.

Having declared ourselves students, we had to elaborate on where we studied, at which specific university, etc. – this was easy for us, as we had indeed studied there a few years ago. Learning more about us, the "Volga" passenger became more respectful and sympathetic. Upon arrival in Taihuai, he carefully settled us in a decent and inexpensive inn, which welcomed us in the middle of the night, and promised to visit us. He also instructed the driver not to charge us (it turned out he wasn't a passenger at all, but some kind of boss, and the driver obeyed him in everything). Extremely pleased, we soon fell fast asleep in the warm inn, while the snow continued outside.

I won't tell you about how we visited all the most famous Buddhist monasteries of Mount Wutai, including the Pushou nunnery, where we were warmly received by charming nuns, or how we bought two swords at a street stall, or climbed the summit of Mount Wutai's (10,033 feet), getting caught in a snowstorm and barely finding our way down. But it's worth noting that on our first day at Mount Wutai, we faced a real challenge – our night benefactor, with his driver, showed up at our inn and invited us to a restaurant, where they treated us to the best local dishes and local vodka. I must say, this vodka more resembled some kind of rotgut, and we drank it with considerable distaste, but out of respect and gratitude, we couldn't refuse. The boss and the driver also got quite drunk. It took us a long time to recover from that vodka, even requiring a basin at the inn. However, the next morning, we set off to the monasteries, hoping, honestly, that we probably wouldn't see our benefactor again.

But suddenly, a couple of days later, when we were resting at the inn after descending from the summit, he appeared again in the evening, businesslike. And then we heard the following from him:

"You see, my friends, all foreigners here must register with the police – those are the rules, and since I'm the chief of police, you should come to my station tomorrow morning with your residence permits and register. It's a simple formality! I wouldn't have bothered you, but those are the rules, sorry! I have to go now, see you tomorrow morning..."

Stunned, we sat on the kang in our room. What should we do?! Tomorrow morning, as soon as we show our residence permits at the police station, our lie about being poor students will be exposed, and it will be revealed that we are managers of foreign firms, raking in money. We could already imagine the surprised, puzzled, and reproachful face of the police chief. What a loss of face for us, what shame! And how to explain our lie to him? And what kind of suspicions might he harbor about us?

We couldn't bear it. The decision was immediate - by the next morning, before the police station opened for the day, we had to leave the Mount Wutai area and vanish, never to return, at least not until there was a change in the police chief.

On a frosty early morning, having paid our hosts at the inn, we left the town of Taihuai by roundabout routes and took the same road back to Shahe Railway Station (there was no other). Only the trouble was that overnight there had been such a snowfall that the road was covered with a layer of snow 20-25 inches thick, making it impossible to travel by bike or car. Of course, there was no sight of a grader or anything similar – such equipment was extremely rare in China in those years. The weather forecast said there would be a sharp thaw in a day, and the snow would start melting quickly. But we couldn't wait.

Thirteen miles through knee-high and deeper snow, pushing our bikes up to the 8,200 feet-high Hongmenyan pass, then down again through the snow for another six miles on the southern slope until the snow finally gave way, turning into ice, and another six miles of descent on our steel steeds through the ice and slush of the melted snow to Shahe Station - that's what we had to go through. And maybe it was for the best? Otherwise, the black "Volga" might have caught up with us at the pass, who knows?

So, on our second attempt, we finally reached Mount Wutai, visited its monasteries and climbed its summit. And again, we learned a lesson, now of a different kind. Were all our actions correct, or would you have behaved differently in such circumstances? I leave all this to your discretion, wishing you luck if the tires of your steel steed ever leave their mark on the roads and mountains of China.

[1] Primitive buses in 1990s Beijing, angular in shape and very metallic.

[2] Shifu – bicycle repairman.

[3] This expression originates from the mocking underground poems of the Soviet poet Vladlen Bakhnov, which contain the words: "But this beauty is marred by tourists who come here, moral freaks."

[4] Mao - Chinese currency unit, 1/10th of the yuan.

[5] Fanza – a traditional Chinese house, particularly in a village.

[6] Kang - a traditional heated brick bed commonly found in homes in Northern China.

[7] Beijing Municipality's territory is vast - 6,336 square miles - and includes countryside and mountains, where people sometimes even go missing.

[8] Li - a traditional unit of distance measurement in China, approximately equal to 0.3 miles.

[9] Argothou - a Beijing baijiu, a type of Chinese liquor made from sorghum, with an alcohol content of 56%.

[10] Shuoshudì in China refers to professional storytellers who entertained people for money by reciting books.

[11] Emphasizing the importance of coal for industry, they call it "black gold."

[12] Kunlun is a Beijing hotel where gays gathered at the Glass Room discotheque at that time.

[13] Yellow pussies - that's what the lamèidì called prostitutes in their jargon.

[14] Li Kui is the hero of the Chinese medieval novel "Water Margin", notable for his equanimity.

[15] Jin is a Chinese unit of weight, approximately equal to one pound.

About the Author

The author is fluent in Mandarin and lived for thirty years in China, where he practiced martial arts, cycling and mountain climbing, including in Tibet. He is interested in Buddhism and the mysticism of the East, loves nature, action and adventure.